AMERICA ☆ THE ☆ DUTIFUL

An Assessment of
U. S. Foreign Policy

BY

Philip W. Quigg

SIMON AND SCHUSTER
New York

SBN 671-20813-6
Library of Congress Catalog Card Number: 74-139656
Designed by Irving Perkins
Manufactured in the United States of America
Printed by Mahony & Roese, Inc., New York, N.Y.
Bound by H. Wolff Book Mfg. Co., Inc., New York, N.Y.

To:
Debbie and Michael
and their generation

Contents

Preface

LLEWELLYN THOMPSON, who spent six years in Moscow as U. S. ambassador, tells a story of a Russian peasant riding across the steppes on a bitterly cold night and finding at the side of the way a bird, half starved and nearly frozen. The peasant took the bird up into his saddle and warmed him with his hands. Riding on, he chanced to find a dollop of fresh cow dung steaming in the snow. He set the little bird into it and went his way. Soon the bird, warmed by the dung and nourished by the seed it found there, began to sing at the top of its voice. Hearing the bird singing, a wolf came along and ate the bird.

Like so many things in real life, the story is not very satisfactory in itself. But it does have a moral, or rather—with characteristic Russian generosity—it has three. The first moral is: he who gets you into it isn't necessarily your enemy; the second, he who gets you out of it isn't necessarily your friend; and the third moral is: if you're in it up to your neck, don't sing.

Each of these morals has its application to American foreign policy. France, our oldest friend, has given us almost as much trouble as the Russians. Communist China's enormous progress of the fifties was wrecked in the next decade, both at home and abroad, by the foolishness of an old man, Mao Tse-tung, and this may have saved us even more misery in Asia than we have already experienced. Certainly we are in it up to our necks in Vietnam, and anyone who sings, who has the temerity to suggest that the United States has not been consistently ineffectual, arrogant, messianic, imperialistic and immoral, is in danger of being gobbled up by a wolf pack of young people, intellectuals and other disenchanted Americans. He will be accused of writing an apologia, of defending the status quo, of credulity in accepting the propaganda of a corrupt and dishonest government.

The risk is worth running. If the trauma of Vietnam destroys our sense of proportion, if our present disarray of mind and spirit infects the decisions which lie ahead, we will not be in any condition to judge either our interests or our responsibilities. Guilt is a notoriously bad motive for action—or inaction. Reasoned criticism of American foreign policy is being drowned by the cries of *Mea culpa,* and a generation is being brought up to believe that everything this country has done since the Marshall Plan is to be despised. Platoons of critics, not satisfied to question our motives, condemn them out of hand. America, in John Leonard's phrase, has been strip-mining her soul.

There is so much wrong with the United States both at home and abroad that it is easy to fall into the role of undiscriminating—and ultimately destructive—critic. Even with the benefit of hindsight, it is more difficult to suggest how, in a less than ideal world, things might have been done better, or to make the intellectual effort to understand why they were done as they were. Moreover, it is emotionally more satisfying to be a critic than a defender or seeming justifier of what is at best a very mixed record of performance. Skepticism is the hallmark of the intellectual, and to exercise it is his chief delight. This is as it should be. But it is also incumbent upon those who listen to remember that the critic who tells us everything we do is wrong, no less than the official who tells us all we do is right, deserves to be heard with skepticism. This is the more true because the outside critic bears no responsibility, suffers no penalties for mistaken choices and—at least in today's climate—makes no personal sacrifice for his beliefs. He is running with the herd. Indeed, the more outrageous his comments the more attention he receives, as the author of *MacBird* discovered when she portrayed the President of the United States as an assassin. A portion of our people are at the point of believing nothing and anything, depending on the source. Our skepticism has been honed to such a fine point that it has become a destructive weapon.

This book, then, is addressed not to the expert, not to the silent majority and, above all, not to that dwindling minority of Americans who believe that their country is endowed with special virtue; rather, it is addressed to. that other minority—or that part of it still willing to listen—which believes that the United States is inherently aggressive, unprincipled and either incompetent or unsuited to play any responsible role in the world. It is not for those who want bloody revolution, but for dissenters and reformers willing to believe that change within the system is still possible. It is an effort to reduce by a small margin the level of skepticism, to suggest that our performance in the world has not been as crude or vainglorious as it is often painted, and to redirect some of the present criticism into more profitable channels. I do not aspire to provide wholly objective analysis of particular policies or events but to provoke thought about the dilemmas of foreign policy and to challenge some of the criticisms which have been accepted as holy writ by an important segment of our population.

The reader will find that American leaders are rarely referred to by name in this book, on the grounds that Pavlovian reactions to "Truman," "Dulles," "Kennedy," "Rusk," "Johnson" *et al.* set up barriers to fresh thinking. Each name conjures up a stereotyped image which simplifies reality. It was Johnson who led the opposition to American involvement in Vietnam in the fifties; Dean Rusk was once one of the most articulate spokesmen for strengthening the United Nations, though he largely ignored it later; many "new initiatives" taken by incoming Administrations were actually begun in the previous one. Under President Eisenhower, the celebrated general, military spending declined, while under Kennedy—to young people and liberal intellectuals generally the most acceptable of postwar Presidents—defense budgets rose significantly.

Another justification for minimizing political personalities is that it is one of the contentions of this book that the continuity of American policy is far more significant than the differences in Administration or individual leaders. This is not—as some suspect—because the leaders have been entrapped by "the system" but because the objective situation which each President, each Secretary of State, encounters in office restricts his alternatives more than even he supposed would be the case. As Charles Frankel has written, "The most difficult political problems are not political but anthropological. They aren't the products of a 'system,' unless it is the human nervous system and the human burden of history."* Readers who find the early chapters too uncritical are urged to persist, for in later pages they will find fuel for their fires. Nevertheless, for those who start from premises quite different from my own, it will require a large measure of what Learned Hand called "the spirit which is not too sure that it is right."

PHILIP W. QUIGG

New York
June 1970

* Frankel, *High on Foggy Bottom* (New York: Harper & Row, 1969), p. 144.

I

Time, Place and Characters

ONE OF the most distinguished critics of American foreign
policy has written:

> Frenetic preoccupation with foreign quarrels has now
> reached the proportion of a heavy industry in this coun-
> try. . . .
> Is the management of our own affairs so efficient and so
> evidently successful that we may take up the role of showing
> other countries just how to manage their internal economies?
> Have we the economic and military power required to set
> their systems in an order to suit our predilections? . . .
> The destiny of Europe and Asia has not been committed,
> under God, to the keeping of the United States; and only con-
> ceit, dreams of grandeur, vain imaginings, lust for power, or
> a desire to escape from our domestic perils and obligations
> could possibly make us suppose that Providence has ap-
> pointed us his chosen people for the pacification of the earth.

What is of particular interest about this quotation is that it
was written shortly before the Second World War, near the end
of two decades of American isolationism and at a moment
when the majority of Americans were coming to realize for the
first time that our lack of commitment to collective security was

in considerable measure responsible for the approaching war in Europe. Moreover, this passage was written by one of the most respected and influential thinkers of this century, Charles A. Beard (in a little volume called *Giddy Minds and Foreign Quarrels*).

It does not follow that because what Beard wrote in 1939 seems somewhat ridiculous, similar criticism today is mistaken. It does, however, lend perspective in evaluating contemporary comment. Whenever a society is under particular stress, and especially when a reexamination of the accepted verities is most urgently required, rational discussion becomes most difficult to conduct. The generation which fought World War II was brought up to believe that war was the worst of all possible evils. No conceivable set of circumstances could justify a return to the battlefield, which, as World War I demonstrated, accomplished nothing, preserved nothing. From the first invasion of Czechoslovakia, through Munich and the blitzkrieg into Poland and the Lowlands, Americans now in their forties and fifties went through agonies of doubt. As assumptions were reexamined and individual commitments made to America First or Aid to Britain, this country suffered a divisiveness comparable to the split of opinion we have experienced over Vietnam. Lessons unlearned are harder to relearn. If those in positions of responsibility in this country no longer believe that war is the worst of all possible evils, it is because they have seen worse— in the extermination of the Jews in Germany and in the elimination of opposition to the Stalinization of Russia. Experience is not necessarily a sound teacher, but it is an effective one. For good or ill (and there are both), American foreign policy is influenced to this day by a sheaf of earlier lessons: that appeasement is never rewarded; that unpreparedness leads to war; that peace can be achieved only by collective security with firm commitments; that with the decline of the former great powers, it is all the more essential that the United States fulfill world responsibilities; that the Soviet Union is expansionist and aggressively hostile.

These assumptions and others made twenty or more years ago, not "lust for power" or virulent anti-Communism, are the stuff of which policy, even today, is made. It would be reckless to assume that these "lessons" have no validity; they are both true and untrue, in varying degrees. And they cannot be ignored, particularly in a democracy, where foreign policies require public support. Nor are these assumptions the vague imaginings of Americans alone; they have been shared in great measure by our allies. As this is written, word comes of the death of Halvard Lange, Foreign Minister of Norway for twenty years. A Socialist and pacifist, son of a recipient of the Nobel Peace Prize, he tried for several years after the war to find a mediating role for Norway between the Soviet Union and the United States. But in 1949, convinced of Soviet intransigence and profoundly disturbed by the incorporation of Czechoslovakia into the Soviet sphere, he felt compelled to urge that his traditionally neutral country join NATO.

At about the time that Charles Beard was castigating the United States for its frenetic preoccupation with foreign quarrels, a group of equally luminous intellectuals, both American and European, were meeting to discuss the implications of the gathering storm in Europe. In 1940, with Europe at war, seventeen of them, including Reinhold Niebuhr, Lewis Mumford, Thomas Mann, Alvin Johnson and Hans Kohn, issued an impassioned document which called for "a Pax Americana" for the benefit of all humanity.

> It is this country virtually alone that carries man's burden.
> . . . Here, and here alone, the continuity of ancient and
> modern wisdom lives. . . . Here . . . the treasure of Eng-
> lish culture is guarded, as Hellenism was preserved in Rome;
> and along with it the treasure and essence of all human cul-
> tures. Here, and almost nowhere else, is Europe: the Europe-

America that will become "all things to all men" to "save them all." . . . Nothing could be more shocking to America's humility and pride than the necessity to take leadership among nations. Much of the charm and fluency of her life, much of her self-assured detachment, will be gone. And yet no necessity is more imperative. . . . Leadership, to be sure, implies some sort of imperium. But there is a difference between imperialism and imperium, between those whom their own lust for power chooses for a self-appointed primacy which is the right of might and those who are chosen by the objective circumstances of history for a privilege which is a service, for a right which is a duty. This is indeed the substance of a chosen people: power in the frame of service.*

How antique these words sound today! And how profoundly some who signed their names to them now disagree. Yet whatever one's quarrel with the authors, they were incontestably correct in assuming that after the war there would be no one else to carry responsibilities formerly borne by the European powers.

Charles E. Bohlen, a man with forty years of experience in the Foreign Service and one of our most knowledgeable students of the Soviet Union, is one who believes our assumption of worldwide responsibilities after World War II and since was necessary and inescapable. Speaking of the network of treaties of mutual security which we forged in the late forties and early fifties, he writes:

It was not a planned operation. It was not even a sought-after operation. It certainly was not done in response to any material need of the United States. The United States needed no more territory. Economically it could assure its needs through the normal processes of trade. It was certainly not due to any American ambition, nor any American wish. It was simply an American response to an external situation which had developed as a result of the war. It was perfectly

* Agar, *et al., The City of Man* (New York: Viking, 1940), pp. 14, 61, 64 and 70-71.

apparent that unless the United States took up the challenge, a large part of the world would fall prey to totalitarian power. There was an element of self-interest in it, but I think also there was a good deal of the element of the feeling of duty toward the civilized world, as it then was. And one of the difficulties of explaining this policy even in the early days, and even more now, is that our policy is not rooted in any national material interest of the United States, as most foreign policies of other countries in the past have been.*

These too are somewhat old-fashioned notions, especially the idea that the United States may have acted out of a sense of duty or in behalf of an interest that was not purely national. Similarly, a President of the United States, at Catholic University, spoke of our "deep and flowing springs of moral duty." This is the kind of rhetoric that infuriates critics and not without reason. Our moralistic bent can lead to hypocrisy and worse. But the substance cannot be dismissed so easily. Our sense of "moral duty" has also benefited mankind; the absence of that cynicism with which older societies view the world, the expectation that we can make it a better place, has caused us to become involved where others would have refrained—and where sometimes we should have refrained. But is it so self-evident, as some suppose, that involvement and commitment, which are considered virtues in interpersonal relations, are to be deplored in international relations? Moreover, we cannot avoid coping with the paradox that among critics with generally similar values and predispositions some want greater morality in our foreign policies, while others believe that our inclination to moralize issues is the cause of our overbearing stance in the world. By defining our national interests more realistically, the latter believe, we would avoid what Ronald Steel has called "welfare imperialism" and what Noam Chomsky has called our "unconstrained viciousness."

* Bohlen, *The Transformation of American Foreign Policy* (New York: W. W. Norton, 1969), pp. 95-96.

Our society today is full of paradoxes. Those who most profoundly abhor the notion that one race is inferior to another are prepared to condemn a whole nation as inherently evil; those Americans who most want power for themselves want the United States to have as little as possible; those who argue against foreign involvements because we cannot foresee their consequences make no effort to examine the possible consequences of our becoming uninvolved; those who are most passionately ideological condemn any suggestion of it in the United States. The list could be extended almost indefinitely. Even the symbols we use are paradoxical and emphasize the chasm between generations: the famous "V for victory" sign that Winston Churchill made known to the world is now the symbol of peace, the peace that everyone wants and that is never finally secured.

Because Americans start from such a variety of premises, what we say to each other often seems totally irrelevant. Even the harshest critics of U. S. foreign policy often reach similar conclusions by surprisingly varied routes reflecting a wide divergence in assumptions. It is not surprising, then, that those who are disposed to find some merit in what the United States has done over the past quarter century have difficulty communicating with those who take the opposite view. Each feels the other has wholly lost his sense of objectivity. Faced with the more extreme denigrators, the defender is reduced to wondering how the motives of American decision-makers can be so consistently bad, while those of others are presumptively so good.

One can, however, distinguish two general schools of thought among those who condemn American foreign policy, not merely in Vietnam but everywhere. The first holds that from its inception the United States has been expansionist, rapacious and guided exclusively by commercial interests—all wrapped in the delusion that what is good for the United States is good for the world. With members of this school it is difficult to find common ground for discussion, for, short of revolution which would alter every value and tradition, we are condemned to proceed on our covetous, imperial way. Yet this school of thought has profoundly affected the generation now reaching maturity. Many of our most intelligent and active students are convinced that the United States has no relationships abroad that are of mutual benefit, none that serve any interest save American business or national security, narrowly and hysterically defined.

The second school holds that the historical record is uneven and that in the postwar years the United States through, say, the end of the Marshall Plan acted with some magnanimity and awareness of our real national interests, despite errors of judgment and exaggeration of the Communist danger. Since then, this school contends, the United States has betrayed its ideals and lost the respect it once deserved by becoming rigid, high-handed and power-mad. With those who take the second view, the dissenter can have a rational discourse, agreeing with them on some specific points while trying to win acknowledgment that power does impose responsibilities and that the question is how we can better define and fulfill those responsibilities, not escape from them.

Some of the basic differences between critics and defenders (using the latter term broadly; we are all critics in fact and at heart) arise from differing conceptions of the world and our power to influence it. It is one of the premises of this book that we live in a dangerous world, which would not be made less threatening by, for example, unilateral disarmament or withdrawal. Since 1945 there have been some fifty-four armed conflicts of sufficient intensity to be classified as wars.* Obviously, the major powers were involved in a small minority of these, so it may be safely assumed that if the United States and the Soviet Union did not exist it would still be a dangerous world, with or without nuclear weapons. Indeed, it is not impossible that it would be a more dangerous world, for the superpowers in some degree have kept a lid on the levels of violence that

* Lincoln P. Bloomfield and Amelia C. Leiss, *Controlling Small Wars: A Strategy for the 1970's* (New York: Knopf, 1969), p. 4.

could be tolerated. Nevertheless, the United Nations estimates that more than half a million Sudanese have been killed in a civil war of which the world knows little and appears to care less. More than 300,000 were killed in Indonesia in October 1966, when an attempted Communist coup was suppressed. In a few days in northern Nigeria, perhaps thirty thousand Ibos were slaughtered, and the human cost of the civil war that followed may not be known for at least a generation. These are events in which the United States played no part; they are mentioned only as a reminder that the sentimental view of the world which holds that man is naturally innocent and only power corrupts is not very persuasive.

Another premise, with which few would disagree, is that domestic and foreign affairs are intertwined more than ever before in our history. In many respects they are hardly separable. It is not merely that the war in Vietnam creates and serves to justify violence at home. More important in the long run is that how we cope with our domestic problems in large measure determines our effectiveness abroad. The whole world is looking at us as at no other nation. This is partly because what we are and do is important to so many, partly because what we do or fail to do is incomparably visible. Moreover, we are judged by different standards than our adversaries, for the test is how close we come to, how far we fall short of, what we ourselves profess. Thus many of our failures of leadership on the world stage have occurred at home rather than abroad. There is simply no end to the ways in which our performance—in race relations or inflation, in technology or balance of payments—affects other people and thus helps or hinders the conduct of our foreign policy.

Yet our shortcomings at home must not be used as an excuse for evading international responsibilities abroad. Many critics contend that we consistently overestimate our capacity to shape the world to our liking and that our efforts to do so turn out to be neither in our interests nor in the interests of those we seek to help. There is much truth to this, but perhaps less than the war in Vietnam has caused us to believe. When historians look back on these decades, one of the wonders to record will surely be the fact that with consistency, generosity and remarkable unanimity, this nation sought to build another federated state potentially its equal in strength and power. For this the historians will not likely find a precedent. There will be nothing quite comparable to the United States—through five Administrations, representing both parties—helping Europe to rebuild and to unite. No one would suggest that it was a purely selfless act or that we had nothing to gain from Europe's revival and integration in greater strength than it had ever known. But in the history of diplomacy it has not been the practice of states to assist in the creation of rivals in economic and military power.

But this we did. And we did it—despite what some of our critics say—without exerting undue pressure, but by encouraging an indigenous movement, by giving Europeans the means and by protecting them from their enemies during the process. That the effort has been only partially successful does not detract from its uniqueness or preclude its ultimate accomplishment.

Not surprisingly, critics hold the United States responsible for what goes wrong, but assume that what goes right happened in spite of us or by virtue of some natural law which we could not affect. To take one dramatic example, C. P. Snow in 1960 lent the vast prestige of science, and of his name, to the assertion that if disarmament was not achieved, nuclear disaster "within at the most ten years" was "a certainty."* He repeated the word four times for emphasis. Within their own discipline, scientists are not wont to use such words lightly. Therefore, are we not justified in believing that it is no small accomplishment to have avoided nuclear war? Some will say it has been sheer luck, but it is strange how rarely in international affairs luck is credited with playing a part except when it is good. Critics say, "We

* Address before the American Association for the Advancement of Science, excerpted in *The New York Times,* Dec. 28, 1960.

were lucky to get out of the Dominican Republic with our skins." But imagine a government spokesman saying, "We have had very bad luck in Vietnam" (which is true). He would be howled down.

Others remark how lucky we were in the Cuban crisis, when the Soviet Union installed offensive missiles contrary to its given word. It has become fashionable in some circles to credit Mr. Khrushchev with "statesmanship" for agreeing to withdraw the missiles. But Russians, high and low, did not consider any part of the adventure statesmanlike, and the incident speeded Khrushchev's demise. Meanwhile, no one has suggested how the United States, so generally criticized for lack of restraint, could have handled the crisis with more steadiness or skill.

Much the same can be said for the handling of the several crises over Berlin, where we were acting in cooperation with Britain and France, but where the initiative and the ultimate power to act were largely ours. The Soviet effort to close off Berlin from the West by threat of force was met by the most cautious response consistent with the West's resolve to protect Berlin. At a time when we had overwhelming nuclear superiority, we yet avoided confrontation. Rather than sending tanks down the autobahn, we simply overflew the Soviet barrier and by a herculean effort supplied Berlin by air. This was not the action of a nation captivated by its own power. It was an action which combined resolution with imagination and restraint.

Three years before Professor Beard wrote his broadside, we had granted self-government to the Philippines, and independence was imminent—though in the event, it was delayed by the war. In those years, this was without precedent. The seizure of the Philippines from Spain was not the happiest chapter in our history, but it hardly bears out the contention that we have a natural imperial bent. We undertook it with no particular enthusiasm and never developed the emotional attachment to the Philippines that a Frenchman felt for Indochina or a Hollander felt for Indonesia. Within eighteen years we had granted the

Filipinos full control of their own legislature, and independence was granted with almost none of the agitation which was applied to colonial powers elsewhere. What the Filipinos resented was not that we oppressed them but that we were so uninvolved. Their dependence upon us became not only economic but emotional. When Manuel Quezon, the first President under the self-governing commonwealth, was trying to develop a sense of Filipino nationalism, he once exploded, "Damn the Americans! Why don't they tyrannize us more?"*

If our role in Puerto Rico has been imperial, surely it is to be marveled at that when Puerto Ricans went to the polls in 1967 to determine their future status, only one percent voted for independence. Indeed, commonwealth status would seem to give Puerto Ricans the best of all possible worlds: self-government with most of the advantages of U. S. citizenship but without paying U. S. taxes. Nevertheless, in the 1967 election 39 percent favored statehood, and the figure is believed to be growing. What is perhaps most remarkable is that, barring some unforeseen resistance, the Puerto Ricans can have any status they want, any time they want, without regard for what may be in the best interests of the United States. If we were the rigid economic determinists that we are so frequently painted, we would have insisted long ago on Puerto Rican independence, for that island of people and poverty is a net loss to us.

Our latest colonial acquisition seems to be almost unnoticed by those who are most concerned about our imperial inclinations. The Trust Territory of the Pacific Islands, more generally known as Micronesia, is composed of former Spanish possessions, later purchased by the Germans and taken from them after World War I to be administered by the Japanese under a League of Nations mandate. Since World War II, we have administered these scattered islands under a United Nations trusteeship. With less than a hundred thousand people dotted

* Quoted in Theodore Friend, "Goodbye, Mother America: An Overview of Philippine–American Relations, 1890–1969," *Asia,* Summer 1969, p. 8.

over an area (mostly water) the size of the United States, Micronesia presents formidable problems of administration and development. Our performance has been mixed, and close study should be rewarding to those interested in examining a genuine American dependency. The Micronesians already have a considerable measure of self-government, and when within a few years they are given an opportunity to choose their future status, they will most likely opt for a relationship with the United States like that of Puerto Rico.

These are not, however, the matters of which Charles Beard was writing. He was concerned to keep us out of an impending war in Europe, just as today's critics are primarily dedicated to getting us out of the war in Vietnam. But men and circumstances change. One of the interesting features of Beard's attack is his acid criticism of one who in his later years has been vehement in the view that the United States is outrageously overcommitted abroad.

> Some of our fellow-citizens [Beard wrote in 1938] of course do not believe that America can deny or refuse to accept the obligation of directing world destiny. Mr. Walter Lippmann is among them. "Our foreign policy," he has recently said in a tone of contempt, "is regulated finally by an attempt to neutralize the fact that America has preponderant power and decisive influence in the affairs of the world. . . . What Rome was to the ancient world, what Great Britain has been to the modern world, America is to be to the world of tomorrow. . . . We cling to the mentality of a little nation on the frontiers of the civilized world, though we have the opportunity, the power, and the responsibilities of a very great nation at the center of the civilized world."

And as if this were not sufficiently apropos of the present day, one final sentence from Beard: "Walter Lippmann says that Americans are suffering from 'a national neurosis,' defeatism, and 'wishing to escape from their opportunities and responsibilities.' "

Thus do things remain the same, even when some of the characters change their viewpoints. The debate over what our proper role in the world should be is not new, having begun with George Washington's first inaugural. It is both understandable and appropriate that the debate should be particularly intense at this time when we are disillusioned by Vietnam and conscious of the need to reexamine our premises and priorities. What is disturbing about much current comment is that it seems to analyze not what our responsibilities are but how we can contract out of them. Those who see our blunders in Vietnam in moral terms and wish to retreat in sackcloth and ashes ignore the needs of a world smoldering with tensions and functioning at a fraction of its capacities. Those who see our failures as purely political and military and who now wish to redefine our national interest in the narrowest possible terms are taking a perilously parochial view of the world. Together they are denying responsibilities and necessities which we have long accepted, which others expect of us, and which Vietnam has in no way altered.

This is not to argue for "globalism," "interventionism," being "the world's policeman" or any of those other wearisome terms with which our domestic critics have flagellated us all for so long. It is to suggest that we now have the possibility of achieving a more realistic view of our capacity to shape the world we live in, a better sense of our limitations and capabilities. Twenty-five years ago we broke out of isolation with energy and optimism, but with no particular satisfaction in the responsibilities that had befallen us. Having adjusted to the idea that the world needed leadership and a part of our wealth, we plunged into the business of giving both with energy and remarkable continuity. If we also had some illusions about the real world and our ability to affect it, we have been given good reason to shed them and to gain a new sense of proportion. We will not gain it by assuming that everything we have done in the past quarter century is reprehensible.

II

The Arrogance
of Impotence

ALL OF us have something in common with the patient taking
a Rorschach ink-blot test: "Why," he asked the psychologist,
"do you show me all these sexy pictures?" We all see what we
are disposed to see. And in so complex and frustrating an arena
as international affairs, where human fallibility seems to find
special nourishment, it is not surprising that we can all find
what we are looking for. The first requirement is that we make
the necessary effort to see more than one thing, one quality.
Generalization is an essential tool of constructive thought, but
the sweeping generalization swung like a medieval flail becomes
a destructive weapon.

Such is the accusation that the United States is arrogant and
messianic. No nation with such a preponderance of power can
expect to escape the charge of arrogance on occasion, and
sometimes it will surely be deserved. What we do—or fail to
do—has so profound an effect on so many nations and peoples
that it would be surprising if some did not think us arrogant.
Among the hundreds of thousands of Americans overseas, there
are bound to be some who are arrogant in word or deed, and
the tendency of our armed forces to live in American enclaves
is often resented. Undoubtedly the worst offenders of foreign

sensibilities are members of Congress who are concerned with winning votes at home, not friends overseas. Yet, strangely, until the term was popularized in the United States, primarily by Senator J. William Fulbright in his book *The Arrogance of Power,* * there is no record of the word being applied to us by foreigners. Frequent travelers abroad were accustomed to being told that we were foolish, wrongheaded, moralistic, heavy-handed, naïve, ill-informed, materialistic, aggressive and a host of other things, but "arrogance" was not in the foreigner's lexicon until American critics made it part of the anti-American vocabulary.

This is not really so surprising. As a people we tend to be unpretentious and well liked. As tourists we have grown more sophisticated, more sensitive to the feelings of our hosts and less vulgar in flaunting our wealth. Though we are known to be proud of our technological achievements and impatient with inefficiency (less so as we have become more aware of our own), we are less haughty than the British, less demanding than the Germans, less self-righteous than the Indians. Unlike the French and the Chinese, we do not think that our culture is the only one of any value. In brief, whatever our shortcomings, arrogance is not a natural characteristic.

This contention is further borne out by our reputation for being among the most self-critical of people. We are a nation of committees and commissions set up to analyze our errors or to establish new goals. Moreover, we are known for our willingness to accept, even welcome, criticism from others. In no other country in the world can a foreigner make a small fortune on the lecture circuit telling his audiences how bad the Americans are—and be lionized in the process.

Our excesses of self-criticism are now a matter of comment abroad. A British scholar-journalist wrote recently:

> Professor Sacher V. Scapegoat, on vacation or sabbatical over here, has long been a figure of terror in London. He

* New York: Random House, 1967.

glazes eyes and makes jaw muscles crack with politely re-
pressed yawns at his tales of how corrupt, how imperialist,
how rich, how unutterably vile his country is. . . . The lu-
nacy most Europeans see in the United States is precisely that
of the Americans who press exaggerated claims for their
country's supreme criminality and unpopularity.*

Finally, we are a nation that cares intensely—too intensely—
what others think of us. This quality is the very antithesis of
arrogance. After twenty-five years' experience, some of the
most influential members of Congress still believe that our overseas programs are, or ought to be, designed to win friends, and
they never cease to be chagrined and annoyed by failure. The
arrogant man or nation does not care about such things; his
sense of innate superiority puts him above such superficial
needs as popularity. The United States has never been a self-
confident nation; indeed, much of the tone of moralism which
irritates many at home and abroad derives in large part from
our constant need to reassure ourselves that we are "doing the
right thing." Other nations at the height of their power never
felt required to justify their every act in rich and rhetorical
detail.

By what measure and from what standpoint are we to be
judged arrogant? Is it in style or the substance of our policies
or both? In an ideal world, leadership would be assigned by a
better criterion than power. And not even the most hard-nosed
official in Washington supposes that our power endows us with
special virtue. What he does suppose—indeed, knows—is that
while other nations may defer decisions or believe that what
they do does not matter, the United States has no such option.
Everything we do or fail to do matters intensely to all, and it is
from this, not free choice, that our responsibilities derive. And
despite all the accusation of our failure to consult or to show
sufficient sensitivity to the interests of others—much of which

* Robert Conquest, "The American Psychodrama Called 'Everyone Hates
Us,' " *The New York Times Magazine,* May 10, 1970.

is justified—our allies have been most unhappy when we led too little rather than too much.

The extent to which our power and wealth places us involuntarily in a special category is easily illustrated. Any international undertaking that costs money must have our support, because we regularly pay between one third and one half the costs. Or, in quite a different area, on repeated trips to Germany, including his triumphal visit after he returned to the presidency of France, Charles de Gaulle never went to Berlin; Germans could interpret this slight any way they wished. But if any high-ranking American official on a trip to Germany had failed to go to Berlin to renew American support of its defense, the panic, the outcry throughout the Federal Republic would have been indescribable. Or again, when Rhodesia took the final step of becoming a republic and leaving the Commonwealth, there were about a dozen foreign consulates in Salisbury, but only the American appeared to matter, either to the illegal white Rhodesian government, to the black African states or to the rest of the world. What might seem like a small matter to us was desperately important in Africa. All the pressures were on the United States, and everyone waited to see what it would do. When the American consulate was closed (as it should have been), all the other countries followed suit. Time and again, what others are free to do, we are not; time and again, the initiative is left to us and others follow.

Foreigners generally seem more willing than American critics to acknowledge that no nation with such a preponderance of power has ever used it with so much restraint and discrimination. In the light of history, this may not be much of an achievement, and it has unquestionably been tarnished in Vietnam. But it should not be ignored. "America has never demanded subservience," a British observer has written. "Indeed much of its help has been specifically designed to promote the independence of other nations singly or in concert."*

* Colin Welch in *The Daily Telegraph*, London, reprinted in *Atlas*, January 1967, p. 45.

Even in Vietnam our difficulties stemmed not from the arrogance of power but from its opposite: failure to insist upon the South Vietnamese making reforms which we initially set as a condition for our aid. From Diem onward, we allowed almost every South Vietnamese leader in effect to blackmail us into a greater commitment without implementing those reforms which we had defined as essential to any measure of success. Arrogance should be made of sterner stuff. And, it may be added, "puppets," as Diem, Ky, Thieu and company have been branded, should be made of more pliable stuff. Time and again we erred on the side of restraint in imposing our views, with the result that no political basis for "victory" was achieved, while we increasingly took over the burden of fighting the war. Of all our sins of omission and commission in Vietnam, arrogance is among the least.

This view has been well expressed by Robert Scalapino:

> . . . One of the chief defects of American policies in Asia has perhaps been the general absence of tough-minded, quid pro quo policies in which all parties to the agreement understand clearly that its success depends upon each playing his role, and further, that the obligations of one party are conditional upon the actions of the other. The charge that the American problem has been an arrogance of power entirely misses the mark, in my opinion. Rather, our problem has been a considerable softness and indecision about how to use the massive power at our disposal. If this has led to "over-Americanization" in some settings because we did not know how to involve and hold responsible those supposedly being helped, it has also frequently led to excessive indulgence with those we are seeking to aid. . . .
>
> This is not a recent problem. Indeed, it has plagued our foreign aid programmes in a number of areas for many years. Nor is it, as some of our critics allege, a manifestation of American imperialism. Ironically, it is much more a manifestation of American liberalism. . . .[*]

[*] Robert A. Scalapino, "American Policy in East Asia," the 1968 Dyason Memorial Lectures, published in *Australian Outlook,* December 1969, p. 262.

Consider our next most disastrous foreign-policy failure—the Bay of Pigs. Was this the failure of an arrogant nation or of one unsure of itself and diffident in the exercise of overt power? An arrogant nation would have overwhelmed so small but threatening an enemy before it could have become dangerous. Our irresolution led to the worst of all possible compromises—to assume responsibility for the intervention of others and without the force necessary to assure success.

One of the fundamental and unavoidable difficulties in our relationship with other nations is the extent to which they look upon the United States as a *deus ex machina* capable of solving all problems if only it had the will and saw the justice of some particular cause. Rare is the Washington official who has so exaggerated a notion of American power as do ministers and heads of state in many countries. "If only the United States would do so and so," they say, and there follows a discourse on how a shift in American policy or tactics would be advantageous to them. Of course, the change might be highly distasteful to their neighbor or it might be wildly inconsistent with other American policies. Of the 120 or so countries with whom we have relations, scores endow the United States with an importance to them that is out of all proportion. To give an extreme illustration, about 60 percent of the officers in the Mexican Foreign Ministry work on United States affairs, 20 percent on international-organization affairs, 15 percent on European affairs and 5 percent on all the rest of the world, including Latin America. This pattern is followed in lesser degrees throughout Latin America and other parts of the world.

It is precisely these attitudes that feed anti-Americanism, which domestic critics tend to assume is a response to our arrogance. We are enjoined to heed what is said of us or done to us abroad, and so we should. But we must seriously distinguish between what is rooted in justified resentment, which we have the means to alter, and that which is an inevitable response to our wealth and power. Anti-Americanism stems much more from what we are than from what we do, and it will not cease with a change in our policies. We are too convenient a scape-goat both for governments and for groups. In addition to the fact that the rich and strong can never escape envy and resent-ment of their good fortune, the United States for many peoples symbolizes the dominance of Western culture, so that we be-come a magnet for unfocused resentment. The harsh rub of cul-tures which is occurring almost everywhere is profoundly up-setting to traditional societies which want the good things that modern technology brings but not the bad.

Few countries have produced more violent demonstrations against the United States than Japan and the Philippines. Yet in both, public-opinion polls regularly indicate that Americans are the most-admired foreigners. This does not mean that all those who like us also like the policies of our government or that other peoples do not have legitimate grievances against us. But if we are overly influenced by demonstrations of anti-Americanism, if we allow them to become an excuse for withdrawal (which may or may not be sound on other grounds), we will merely be showing "a need to be loved" that is charac-teristic of immaturity. Given the number of protest demonstra-tions around the world that are wholly unspontaneous, indeed are bought and paid for, they are hardly a guide even to pub-lic opinion, much less to policy. When one considers in how many countries anti-Americanism is conducted as a systematic campaign by government-controlled press and radio, the won-der is that it has been relatively so ineffectual. Anti-American-ism is as often a device for stimulating national unity as it is a true reflection of public opinion.

Two minor instances illustrate how difficult it is to hold pop-ularity abroad. When war broke out between El Salvador and Honduras, the United States took the position that the dispute should be settled primarily by the five Central American repub-lics with the good offices of the Organization of American States. For this evidence of detachment and non-involvement, the Hondurans, who were not a match for the El Salvadoreans, were angry with the United States and showed it by allowing a crowd to smash windows of a U. S. consulate while the police stood by. They said the United States had let them down, that it could and should have halted the war. Should we take this sort of demonstration seriously?

When the Okinawans were agitating for reversion to Japan, it was repeatedly pointed out to them that this would almost certainly mean a gradual reduction in jobs provided at the U. S. bases. Shortly after we had agreed to return political and administrative control of the island to Japan in 1972, with limitations on our base rights, a small number of Okinawans were laid off work at one of the bases. The Okinawans protested vehemently and went out on strike to enforce their demands that no jobs be eliminated. Having demonstrated repeatedly for reversion, they will now increasingly demonstrate against its inevitable consequences.

All of this is natural and understandable, but it requires that we keep a sense of proportion about the alleged animosity the world feels for us and examine the specific causes of anti-Americanism with an open mind. Some things we could do to alleviate it before demonstrations occur; others are built into the situation and we will have to learn to live with them.

Anti-Americanism is as likely to arise from what we don't do as from what we do. With varying emphasis, almost every country wants to have a special relationship with the United States, and this applies even to our "enemies." Each country wants us to recognize its special character, its special needs, the reasons why it is uniquely deserving of aid or preference. This is particularly marked in Latin America, partly because we tend to treat it as an entity despite its enormous national differences, and partly because of our presumed importance to its welfare. Until recently, the nations of Latin America had extraordinarily little contact with one another and each felt it had little to learn from, and little in common with, others. Their ignorance of one another has been profound—far greater than our ignorance of them.

Under these circumstances, it is very difficult indeed to avoid

the appearance of arrogance. If a government official sometimes seems unaware or insensitive to accusations against the
United States, it may be because he just spent a morning with
a prime minister who flattered the United States and urged its
representative not to believe the derogatory things that he felt
obliged to say in public.

To be sure, we have often used the leverage of our wealth
and power in ways which could be interpreted as arrogant,
whether or not that term was used. In the immediate postwar
years, the colonial powers resented our pressure to permit self-
determination to their subject peoples. The French objected to
our unwillingness to give them total support in North Africa,
though we went further than we wanted to in order to avoid
French obstruction in Europe. The British resented our ad-
monishments with respect to Iran, where the stubborn resistance of the Anglo-Iranian Oil Company to any concessions to
Persian nationalism was driving Iran straight into the hands of
the Communists. These few examples among many illustrate
the importance of distinguishing the mere fact of pressure from
the purposes for which it is applied. In retrospect, these purposes appear justified, though it is those which may not have
been that tend to be remembered. Sometimes, too, the pressures we applied were welcomed by foreign governments in that
they strengthened their hand in moving in directions which they
recognized as desirable, though not necessarily popular.

One of the principal issues on which we were criticized for
being too vehement was the so-called Multi-Lateral Force
(MLF), a scheme for joint NATO operation of Polaris submarines with mixed crews. Therefore, let us examine it briefly.

The designers of the MLF were looking for something which
ideally would have these attributes: It would give the Europeans a greater sense of participation in the planning of their
own defense and at the same time expose them to some of the
problems and responsibilities of a nuclear defense, including
targeting, command and control. It would discourage the pro-

liferation of nuclear weapons by reducing the temptation to create independent national nuclear forces; in particular, it would reduce any latent desire of Germany to become a nuclear power, a possibility that frightens all Europeans and would drive the East European satellites pell-mell back into a rigid Soviet bloc. This ideal creation also would stimulate a sense of Atlantic community and counter tendencies toward a Third Force in Europe, and it would strengthen the concept of collective security by establishing the basis of a truly integrated defense.

Now, it is hardly surprising that no wholly adequate answer was found. But the MLF touched all these bases. The idea originally was offered very tentatively and long after the Europeans had failed to come up with any proposal of their own. Indeed, as late as September 1962, when the President's Special Assistant for National Security Affairs addressed the Atlantic Treaty Association at Copenhagen, he did not talk about the MLF. On the contrary, he said that although the United States favored a NATO solution, if the Europeans wanted their own nuclear force, separate from ours but genuinely multilateral, we would not stand in their way. Indeed, we would cooperate in bringing it into being. Does this sound like arrogance?

As long, then, as it appeared that Europe was moving toward greater unity, all options were open. But when Britain was excluded from the Common Market in January 1963 and it appeared that Europe would be permanently divided between the Six and the Seven,* Washington began to believe that something like the MLF was essential. Nearly two years after the idea had been proposed, the United States started to press for its acceptance, while continuing to show a willingness to

* The Six (nations of the European Economic Community) are France, Germany, Italy, Belgium, Holland and Luxembourg; the Seven (nations of the Free Trade Association) are the United Kingdom, Sweden, Denmark, Norway, Austria, Switzerland and Portugal. If Britain is admitted to the EEC it is expected that others of the "Seven" will follow.

alter it in several particulars—as in fact it was altered. Ulti-mately, the plan was in effect rejected, as in all probability it deserved to be. The MLF was perhaps an unsatisfactory com-promise between the Europeans' desire for some control over nuclear weapons and acts of Congress requiring that warheads be kept under an American key. But since no one had a better idea, and since it represented a conscientious effort to be re-sponsive to European desires, it is difficult to understand why some Europeans became so exercised. The United States had nothing to gain from the project except the evidence it might suggest of Atlantic solidarity. The MLF may have been pushed too hard, but it was not conceived in arrogance.

The Latin Americans do have some basis for believing we are arrogant, for we are undoubtedly impatient with their ap-parent incapacity to govern themselves, their unwillingness to take actions which seem so patently necessary, and their ex-tended failure to capitalize on their substantial human and ma-terial resources. The Latin Americans feel economically and culturally superior to Africa and Asia and do not like to be lumped with the Third World. Yet they have probably accom-plished less than Africa and Asia in terms of what they have to work with. If we are arrogant toward our southern neighbors today, however, we were far more so in the past; that is, we were more arrogant when we had less power. Admitting our ag-gressions and transgressions of the past and our frequent prac-tice of a might-makes-right philosophy, nevertheless, there is hardly a constructive move we can make in Latin America without opening ourselves to the charge of arrogance. We are accused by rightists and leftists alike of failing to give adequate support to them or of interfering in behalf of their opponents. When we tried to disabuse those many Latin Americans who believed that the Alliance for Progress was simply a $10-billion handout imposing no obligations on them, we were accused of "telling them what to do," as we certainly were. Yet if we manifest insufficient interest in Latin America, we are equally vulnerable to criticism. The Latin Americans demand that we take measures to increase trade with them, but they do next to nothing to increase trade with one another, which is even more essential. They demand of us high levels of aid, but make no concerted effort to increase the proportion of domestic resources going into production, as opposed to consumption. To point out these failures is not welcome. One does not, then, have to land troops in the Dominican Republic or twist arms in the Organization of American States to stand accused of arrogance. It is built into the situation.

A severe critic of American foreign policy has acknowledged:

> In their frustration, Latin American reformers berate the United States for not doing what they have been unable to do themselves. Overestimating the purposeful exercise of American power, and confusing the role of American business with that of the American government, Latin Americans see the heavy hand of the United States even where it is not necessarily present. Just as they assume that it is entirely our fault that they live under tyrannical governments, so they imagine that we can dismiss the tyrants at will. They criticize us for interfering in their affairs, and then complain that we do not use our power to achieve objectives which they consider desirable. They want us to solve their problems but to do so without interfering. . . . They want us, in other words, to intervene where it suits their purpose, and not to intervene where it doesn't. They seem to need the United States to rail against as much as to emulate, to provide solutions for their problems and to blame for their own shortcomings.*

In fact, the Latin Americans resent our paternalism more than our arrogance. A distinguished Argentine social scientist has said that even the most leftist North Americans are paternalistic as soon as they get south of the Rio Grande. We have

---

* Ronald Steel, *Pax Americana* (New York: Viking, 1967), p. 245.

been made thoroughly conscious of this fault, but probably shall not master it until the Latins overcome their parochialism. Despite their involvement with the United States, there is little or no systematic study of this country. At universities students can learn little that is contemporary about countries other than their own, and only in the last few years has there been any effort to examine the problems of Latin America on a regional basis. Until very recently there was no Latin-American news service and virtually no reporting of other nations within the continent; newspapers had to rely entirely on U. S. and European wire services. Only now, partly as a result of their resentment of U. S. dominance, the Latin Americans are beginning to develop a continental consciousness and a desire for closer cooperation—economic, political and cultural.

We have many sins to atone for in Latin America, but criticism cannot be a one-way street. Let us by all means set high standards for ourselves and understand how far short we have fallen. Yet we owe it to the Latin Americans to be as candid with them as they are with us. Efforts to ingratiate ourselves with Latin Americans while they use us as a whipping boy for their own failures will serve no useful purpose.

None of this is to say that the Latin Americans do not have legitimate grievances, especially against U. S. commercial interests (see Chapter VII). But many of the things they demand of us, such as removal of all barriers to their manufactured goods and higher prices for their raw materials, will increase their dependence on us at a time when they profess the desire, indeed the necessity, of breaking free of our economic domination. And if they are entitled to make demands on us, as they are, we are justified in making demands on them.

After his extended study of Latin America in 1969, Nelson A. Rockefeller reported to the President that the United States "has underestimated the capacities of these nations and their willingness to assume responsibility for the course of future developments." Quite the opposite may be true. That Latin

America has the requisite talent no one doubts, and for this very reason we have tended to overestimate its capacity to achieve its objectives. It has yet to demonstrate the political will or to find the leadership capable of pushing through even those programs on which there is a substantial consensus. Each failure leads to further loss of self-respect, to heightened sensitivity and enlarged resentment of the United States.

Since we are not discussing absolutes, and since all attributes, especially of nations, are relative, let us look at one of our allies and weigh France in the scale of arrogance. Can anyone seriously argue that the United States since World War II has matched the following record?

France has: defied the nearly unanimous decision of the U. N. General Assembly to halt arms sales to South Africa; joined with the Soviet Union in refusing to pay its pro-rata share of the costs of U. N. operations for which it had voted; broken its agreement to sell fighter planes to Israel and instead sold twice as many to Libya, which cannot fly them and will almost certainly make them available to Egypt if needed; insisted, as a condition for accepting a friendship pact with Germany, that French replace English as the second language taught in German schools; encouraged a part of an allied country, Canada, to secede, and thereafter treated Quebec in several respects as an independent nation; withdrawn its troops from NATO and driven NATO installations from its soil, knowing that for geographic reasons the Alliance has no alternative but to continue to include France in its territorial defense; twice defied the wishes of its Common Market partners in refusing the admission of Great Britain to the European Economic Community, and then (following de Gaulle) set as a condition of British entry that all the other members subsidize indefinitely the enormous inefficiencies of French agriculture; unilaterally defeated the European Defense Community, a setback to integration from which Europe never recovered; become a nuclear power in defiance of the international effort to avoid proliferation, and taken the position that any nation capable of becoming a nuclear power has an obligation to become a nuclear power; fought more bloody wars than any other nation in the postwar period, including outright aggression against Egypt; maintained a more overtly colonial position in Africa than any other country; extended needlessly through arms sales Biafra's war of secession, presumably in the hopes of obtaining oil rights there; sought single-handedly to force an increase in the price of gold, which would have benefited only itself and the two major producers, South Africa and the Soviet Union; defeated U. S. efforts to avoid an unnecessary and extravagant arms race in Latin America by selling sophisticated fighter planes there after the United States refused; and threatened to recognize East Germany and withdraw its support for German reunification if Germany joined the MLF.

Even this is not a comprehensive list, but it is enough to show that on the arrogance scale we are lagging. It is also a (non-Communist) reminder that we live in a selfish world, where some countries define their national interest very narrowly indeed. If we cannot (nor want to) claim altruism for ourselves, we can at least assert that we have seen our interests as more broadly corresponding to those of a community of nations.

Indeed, today arrogance seems to be a concomitant not so much of power as of impotence. Witness the language with which little Albania, China's only reliable ally, addresses the Soviet Union, or the terms in which North Korea or Cuba addresses the United States. France was not so arrogant when it was a truly major power, and the Soviet Union has grown slightly less so as its power increased. The truculence with which China addresses the world is surely born of its consciousness of the disparity between its claims to power and its essential weakness.

This raises the interesting question whether the American

people are really conscious of U. S. power, whether they are not far more aware of our inability to use the power we have. To the extent that we have been assertive or arrogant, it is more likely to have stemmed from the frustration we often feel as a result of failures to bring our power to bear for constructive purposes. One of the lessons of recent decades is that in some degree we are all impotent when as nations we act alone; from the poorest to the richest we are all frustrated in reaching our objectives.

Nevertheless, to keep some perspective, we need only ask such questions as: Can anyone imagine the United States announcing unilaterally that its territorial waters extended two-hundred miles to sea, as Peru and now several other countries have done? And, if so, what would the world reaction be? Would an arrogant country agree in time of war to give over to another the civil administration of its largest logistical base (Okinawa)? Would the President of an arrogant power, at some political cost to himself, go to such extraordinary lengths as to make an unscheduled trip to New York to appease the sensitivities of a visitor (President Pompidou), offended by orderly demonstrations?

Another home-grown criticism, allied to the accusation of arrogance, is that the United States is messianic, that it seeks to impose its views and values on the rest of the world. Strangely, this criticism comes from the same people who accuse us of failing to support democracy abroad. What, then, are we messianic about? Far from our imposing our ideas of democracy on the rest of the world, they are sought—in principle if not in fact. To be sure, Africans and Asians speak of adapting Western democracy to their own institutions and the particular genius of their people, and we respond, in the words of our President, by advocating a world made safe for diversity. But when we venture—against our best instincts and beliefs—to agree with those who assert that democracy may indeed be possible in a one-party system, some of the most eminent Africans, including the President of Ghana, reply that we are talking nonsense. And if we go so far as to imply that perhaps a particular country is not ready for democracy, legions rise up to express their sense of outrage. No matter how long a nation's tradition of military government, of coups and dictatorships, to suggest that it is not capable of democracy is considered a mortal insult—and understandably so.

It is true that we have made sustained efforts to promote democratic ideals and institutions in Latin America, where democracy is actually on the wane and where a preference for *caudillo* rule is repeatedly demonstrated. In Colombia, in 1970, after a dozen years of constitutional government and considerable progress, the people came within a hair's breadth of freely electing to the presidency a general who earlier had given Colombia "one of the most savage, venal and altogether incompetent administrations in the history of the nation."* General Gustavo Rojas Pinilla seized power in Colombia in 1953, following years of civil war, and subjected his country to ruthless dictatorship. That he should have succeeded in selling himself in the 1970 election as the friend of the common man is a hideous irony.

Brazil, Argentina, Peru and Uruguay are other countries which in recent years have backtracked from democracy and constitutional government. But very few are free from some degree of political oppression. According to Amnesty International, only Costa Rica is without political prisoners, and the Inter-American Press Association asserts that suppression of newspapers and periodicals is worse than at any time since World War II.

Thus there is very little democracy to support in Latin

---

* Hubert Herring, one of the leading scholars of Latin America, quoted by Malcolm Browne in *The New York Times,* June 9, 1970. It should be added that, although the election is adjudged to have been fair, the final count of the ballots is a matter of dispute.

America, though we have clearly favored and encouraged those countries with constitutional governments and honest elections, even when—as in Chile—we were not happy with the outcome. In most of the continent, we would do well to talk less about democracy, which has acquired a bad name in Latin America, and do more to promote "good government" and "representative government," responsive to the needs and demands of its people.

Is it about capitalism that we are alleged to be messianic? Critics are rarely specific. To be sure, we have businessmen at home and abroad who are zealous in their efforts to promote free enterprise, but most Americans who deal in any capacity with the new nations know that a mix of some kind between socialism and private enterprise is virtually inescapable unless one is prepared to sacrifice development for ideological purity. Governments in the new countries simply do not have the competence to control every aspect of the economy. On the other hand, it is widely recognized that many things that need doing will not get done by private initiative. If we were messianic about capitalism we would not provide economic aid to socialist-minded governments but only to private banks. In fact American capitalism is more regulated and constrained than that of most countries, so that the field of operation for messiahs of free enterprise is somewhat limited. Essentially this issue is a dead horse, and it is paradoxical that those who are now so much concerned with the centralization of power in the U. S. government should still imply that centralization of control is desirable for others.

It is also difficult to reconcile the charge of messianism with the accusation, more common among friends abroad than among Americans, that our ineffectiveness in foreign policy stems from our *lack* of ideology. We carry pragmatism to a fault, it is said, improvising from day to day. Are these the qualities of a messiah?

Finally, the policy of containment can be criticized on many scores, but whatever it is, it is not messianic. If, indeed, containment has been the dominant American foreign policy since World War II, as many critics affirm, then it is a contradiction to assert that we are also messianic. One is the antithesis of the other.

One of the keenest students of the American government has pointed out that inherent in the process of making foreign policy is a tendency toward relativism and that what we need is greater, not less, commitment. And he adds: "Like the historic Episcopalian vexation over what to do with Methodist enthusiasm, professional diplomacy frets over what to do with zeal."*

In late 1967, a group of fourteen distinguished scholars— most of them Asian experts—issued a statement designed to counter the growing hysteria over Vietnam. Not one of the group, which included Edwin O. Reischauer, A. Doak Barnett, Harry D. Gideonse, Oscar Handlin and Lucian Pye, was a defender of U. S. policy in Vietnam, but all felt that the *mea culpas* were becoming excessive and destructive.

> On balance [they wrote] our record in the world, and in Asia since World War II, has been a remarkably good one, worthy of support.
>
> We are capable, moreover, of rectifying mistakes. Among the major societies of this era, the United States has shown a considerable capacity for pragmatism and self-examination, a healthy avoidance of narrow nationalism. If these qualities are to be encouraged, we must challenge those among us who, overwhelmed by guilt complexes, find comfort in asserting or implying that we are always wrong, our critics always right, and that only doom lies ahead.
>
> Our political leaders, our intellectual community, and our mass media each bear heavy responsibilities with respect to these matters. And these responsibilities are not currently being discharged satisfactorily in any quarter.

* Thomas L. Hughes, "Relativity in Foreign Policy," *Foreign Affairs,* July 1967, p. 675.

III

Are We Obsessively
Anti-Communist?

WHETHER ONE believes that our foreign policies have been shaped by an unwarranted fear of Communism will of course depend much on one's concept of Communism and the international aims of those who profess it. But whatever one's view, it should be remembered that in this country fear of Communism is much older than those foreign policies which are now so widely criticized—older indeed than Soviet Communism. A distinction needs to be made between popular American attitudes toward Communism—a factor in the process of making decisions which critics are prone to overlook—and the attitude of those responsible for making policy. Paul Seabury states it accurately when he writes:

> The Cold War as defined by Soviet Marxists and other Communists concerned the future of communism everywhere. Influential American and Western leaders, however, avoided such apocalyptic views of the struggle. . . . In practice, at any given time, Western statesmen tended to stress the Soviet problem, not communism, as the key issue.

On the other hand, he goes on, the public generally perceived "the supreme issue" as "a highly generalized threat posed by communism to an American way of life."*

Thus there has always been tension between the public's view of Communism, broadly reflected in Congress, and the perception of those who were making policy. Dean Acheson, considered by many of today's more extreme critics as the architect of the Cold War, addressed this problem in January 1950:

> I hear almost every day someone say that the real interest of the United States is to stop the threat of Communism. Nothing seems to me to put the cart before the horse more completely than that. . . . Communism is the most subtle instrument of Soviet foreign policy that has ever been devised, and it is really the spearhead of Russian imperialism. . . . It is an important point because people will do more damage and create more misrepresentation in the Far East by saying our interest is merely to stop the spread of Communism than any other way. Our real interest is in those people as people. It is because Communism is hostile to that interest that we want to stop it.†

This distinction is important. Without it we could not have supported Yugoslavia, a state which has never ceased to affirm its dedication to Marxism-Leninism. When Yugoslavia asserted its independence of the Soviet Union in 1950, we quite rationally supported it. Without our aid, amounting to more than $200 million in the first year, it is quite unlikely that Tito would have been successful.

A later observer of international affairs has written:

> . . . the Western posture toward Communism is not one of crusading militancy. The West does not expect to dismantle

<hr />

* Seabury, *The Rise and Decline of the Cold War* (New York: Basic Books, 1967), pp. 83-84.

† Speech before the National Press Club, Jan. 12, 1950, quoted in Hans J. Morgenthau, *A New Foreign Policy for the United States* (New York: Praeger, for the Council on Foreign Relations, 1969), p. 17.

the existing social-political organization of the Communist states, but rather relies primarily on the erosive effects of time and the pressures of change within the Communist states themselves. It therefore does not pose a direct threat to the survival of Communism.*

This expectation of change within Communist states has been a constant theme among the highest officials of the American government. Change there has been, but it would be difficult to argue that expectations have been fulfilled—even those of such Cold Warriors as John Foster Dulles, much less those of that minority who were always disposed to believe the best of the Soviet Union. Indeed, anticipation of change often outran the reality. Because of some moderation in the language with which the Soviet Union expressed its hostility to the United States, it was said in the early sixties that a détente had already set in, that there was no evidence of Soviet expansionism, if there ever had been, and that Communist parties throughout the world were no longer taking orders from Moscow. Then Mr. Khrushchev implanted missiles in Cuba. Those who today insist we have nothing to fear from Communist nations would do well to be a little less certain they are right. Such détente as exists today arises from mutual fear and prudence, not from change in Soviet objectives or resolution of specific issues between the superpowers. Neither détente nor the reputed loss of revolutionary zeal in Moscow saved Czechoslovakia in 1968. In almost every respect the Soviet Union has been betraying the assurances of those who promised that it was becoming more moderate, more permissive, more satisfied with the status quo. In recent years, on the contrary, it has become more vitriolic in its language toward the United States, more repressive toward any forms of dissent, and more expansionist (in the Middle East and the Mediterranean). Even as it overcomes the military superiority we so long enjoyed, the United States reduces its defense budget to the lowest level

* Zbigniew Brzezinski, "Tomorrow's Agenda," *Foreign Affairs*, July 1966, p. 663.

since the Korean War and prepares to reduce its forces not merely in Vietnam, but virtually everywhere. Surely this does not reflect obsessive anti-Communism.

One of the constant dilemmas of our national leaders, and one of their terrible preoccupations, is to present to our antagonists a stance that appears accommodating without appearing weak. It would be nice to believe that we lived in a world where magnanimity was rewarded, but the neighborhood we live in is analogous to a bad ghetto, where the gang that betrays irresolution may invite trouble. Almost all observers agree that the Cuban missile crisis arose out of Khrushchev's misestimation of a young and inexperienced President who, at their meeting in Vienna, was anxious to demonstrate his desire to set a new course in Soviet-American relations. What was intended as a sign of flexibility was read as a sign of weakness, of irresolution. The error was appallingly dangerous, and every President since (as well as those before) has been determined not to give cause for its repetition. This simple fact has perhaps done more than anything else in recent years to give the impression that the United States is irrationally hostile to Communism. Whoever occupies the White House is conscious—much more than his critics—that he simply cannot afford to give the wrong signal: to suggest, for example, that our desire for peace is so overriding that we will not defend our interests and commitments in the Middle East.

Much is made of the fact that the Communist world is no longer monolithic, that in consequence we are less endangered. The point is true but can easily be exaggerated. The greatest change has been upon Communist parties in non-Communist states; they are seriously fractured, and this has weakened them especially in Latin America and India. But polycentrism has not meant that Czechoslovakia represents an independent center of power, as the Russians made pointedly clear in August 1968. Nor has it prevented every Communist state of any consequence from arming and supplying the North Vietnamese for their adventures not merely against South Vietnam but throughout Indochina. And though the hostility that has arisen between China and the Soviet Union may be preferable from our point of view to perfect harmony between them, it is small comfort to see two nuclear powers mustering one and a half million men on their common frontier.

Moreover, none of the issues which brought on the Cold War —the Soviet grip on Eastern Europe, the division of Germany, the status of Berlin, the failure to achieve international control of arms—has been resolved or appreciably ameliorated. It is significant, too, that except for the Sino–Soviet split, the configuration of power and alignment among the major powers has remained remarkably unchanged in twenty years—which suggests that others have seen the world much as we have.

Yet we are earnestly told by one of the new critics that "if America has an ideology, or a national purpose, it is anti-communism."* The writer goes on to paint a picture of national paranoia. If this be true, how, then, did we refrain from exploiting our nuclear monopoly when we had it? Why did we, on the contrary, make a serious effort to internationalize the atom? Why did we disarm after World War II and refrain until the Korean War from building any significant number of atomic bombs? Why did we offer the Soviet Union and Eastern Europe inclusion in the Marshall Plan? How is one to explain the consistency with which we pressed our allies to grant self-determination and independence to their colonies? Surely we understood that they would be prey to instabilities of every kind. Since World War II, some eighty nations representing close to a billion people have achieved independence. This predominantly peaceful transfer of power constituted a revolution the like of which the world had never seen nor will again. It is hard to conceive this happening if the guiding principle of the world's most powerful nation had been fear of Communism.

* Michael Parenti, *The Anti-Communist Impulse* (New York: Random House, 1969), p. 4.

In Laos, we gave our support to Souvanna Phouma at a time when his tolerance of Communism seemed inexhaustible. When there was a leftist revolution in Yemen, supported by the Soviet Union and Egypt, we recognized the regime even before the degree of its popular support had been established and despite the fact that the new government was anathema to neighboring Saudi Arabia, a country whose good opinion is of the greatest importance to us. We gave aid to the leftist regime of Sekou Touré when most people assumed that Guinea was lost to the Soviet Union. We have resisted the notion, so assiduously spread in the United States, that the Republic of South Africa is a bulwark against Communism. Indirectly, we have aided refugees from South Africa whether or not they were Communists. Washington has sustained good relations with Julius Nyerere despite the fact that he has had Communists in his government, that he has thrown out the Peace Corps, and that the largest development project in Tanzania is being conducted by the Communist Chinese. Long before de Gaulle talked about a Europe "from the Atlantic to the Urals," we were seeking to build bridges to Eastern Europe. We have supported and encouraged recent German efforts to reach agreements with the Soviet Union on a bilateral basis. Though many West Europeans have minimized the Soviet threat, it is striking how uneasy they become when the United States enters into negotiations with Russia in an effort to limit armaments. On balance, too, we have shown more willingness, and taken more initiative, to negotiate our differences than have the Soviets.

Each of these instances of flexibility, which critics deny, would seem to contradict the assertions that we are irrationally anti-Communist and unwilling to support left-of-center regimes (see Chapter IV). Each of them had somewhat different origins and expectations, and very few achieved anything like success. The recognition of Yemen was intended to give us more leverage with Nasser, but it only made him more brazen in his efforts to obtain control of the Arabian peninsula. We did well to put confidence in Souvanna Phouma, but our hopes for the neutralization of Laos were destroyed almost as soon as agreement had been reached. This is not to say that these policies were necessarily wrong; but they have not strengthened the hand of those in government who argue for more flexible responses.

If we were as obsessed by Communism as is often charged, we would not have had the capacity to learn and to question past assumptions. And this we have done. For example, we have increasingly appreciated that nationalism is a serious obstacle to Communism except where it is genuinely indigenous, or where it has been imposed by subterfuge from above, as in Cuba—superversion, it has been called, rather than subversion. We have also observed that some societies, notably in Africa, seem impervious to Communism because they simply do not fit the preconceptions of Marxism-Leninism. (Of this we should not be too confident, however; Confucian and Islamic cultures were thought to be immune to Communism and were not.) Or, again, we have increasingly endorsed neutralism, a step that was made easier by the decline in the mystique of nonalignment.*

None of this suggests the inflexibility that has been attributed to the U. S. government by legions of critics. Strangely, even China does not bear out the contention that our government has shown an irrational fear of Communism. Despite the prevalent feeling in America that Communists are unwilling to share power and will always seize total power whenever they can, our government officials, at what proved to be serious risk to their careers, made herculean efforts in the late for-

---

* In 1960, the year of African independence, the President of the United States said in an address to the U. N. General Assembly: "We do not urge—indeed we do not desire—that you should belong to one camp or the other. . . . The only thing we ask is that, through your own love of freedom and the determination of your people to live their own lives as they choose, you will resist others who have military, economic, or political intent to dominate you."

ties to achieve a compromise between the Nationalists and the Communists. General George C. Marshall, later Secretary of State, devoted nearly a year to the effort, and for his pains and fairness he was called a traitor by several Congressmen. Popular passions regarding China were fierce in those days, and they were fed by one of the most powerful lobbies ever marshaled in this country. Those who are lofty in their condemnation of the Washington bureaucracy, and particularly of the State Department, might be more effective if they occasionally acknowledged the acts of political courage that occur there—not often enough, perhaps, but sometimes against enormous pressures.

Parenthetically, it may be pointed out here that, as with so many other issues on which foreign-policy critics wax dogmatic, the democracy which they assert we fail to encourage abroad is a fact at home—at least to the extent that makers of foreign policy are often bound within rigid limits as to what the public will accept. Large numbers of Americans were bitterly disillusioned by the triumph of Communism in China. In what is today known as participatory democracy, they made their feelings felt. Attitudes may have been emotional (as they are today) and sometimes ill-informed, but they were genuine and had little or nothing to do with commercial or strategic interests.

It is generally forgotten that (a) we were contemplating recognition of Communist China in 1949 when Peking arrested and imprisoned the American consul general in Manchuria, and (b) we gave neither support nor protection to Chiang Kai-shek on Formosa until the outbreak of the Korean War, when it seemed necessary to include Taiwan in the Pacific defense perimeter. Even then, the Seventh Fleet, which was sent to the Straits of Formosa to prevent a possible attack by Peking, also had orders to stop any efforts on the part of Chiang to attack the mainland. Despite one brief and ill-advised threat to "unleash Chiang" several years later, this situation has persisted for two decades. It may have outlived its usefulness, but it is more even-handed than is generally acknowledged.

In any event, the Korean War had a profound effect on American attitudes and policies, hardening positions from which we had been prepared to withdraw and leading us to assume obligations in the western Pacific which we had not intended. After China entered the war, any hope of recognition in the near future was removed. Nevertheless, there is substantial evidence that by the middle fifties we would have been prepared to allow the admission of China to the United Nations if Peking had been willing to make the smallest gesture of accommodation—such as the release of American war prisoners, some of whom are being held even to this day.

Those nations who were quick to recognize Communist China and support its admission to the U. N. got little but insults in return. Ambassadors in Peking, whether of the West, of the East or neutral, were isolated and ignored. They obtained little or no information or knowledge of China. Journalists and travelers saw only what the regime wanted them to see, and they were, and remain, in constant danger of abuse and imprisonment. The number of foreign correspondents in Peking, according to Agence France-Presse, has dropped from over forty to fifteen, of whom only three are from Western nations, plus three from Japan. This does not do much for the argument that we should recognize Peking in order to obtain more and better information.

While the United States has been accused of ignoring the most populous nation on earth and pretending it didn't exist, we have in fact been conducting a series of conversations with the Communist Chinese, which have been exceeded in length and importance only by those the Chinese have conducted with the Russians and the Japanese. More than 136 talks have been held over a period of eighteen years, though with long breaks between them and without any evidence that the Chinese are willing to mitigate their hostility to us. Nevertheless, we are trying to persuade the Chinese to conduct these talks on a regular basis. Thus, the oft-repeated charge that "we are the victims of our self-imposed ignorance"[*] is nonsense; the world's ignorance is imposed by China and no nation on earth has made such a systematic effort to overcome this handicap as has the United States. In addition to direct talks, virtually every traveler to China is interviewed and scores of experts in Hong Kong analyze every word appearing in the Chinese press or uttered on Chinese radio and television. That American expertise on China is unequaled is attested to by the fact that scores of Russians now visit this country expressly to consult our China scholars.

It is said that our China policy has been frozen in inertia for two decades. In fact by the early sixties we had moved to a position of favoring contacts and urged upon the Chinese an exchange of scholars and journalists. By the middle of the decade, the American President was speaking of the need for reconciliation with China. More recently the total prohibition on Chinese goods entering this country was lifted, the forces policing the Taiwan Straits were slightly reduced, and the prohibition against the use of American passports for travel to China was removed. Next, the ban was lifted on trade with China by foreign subsidiaries and affiliates of U. S. companies, and somewhat later these subsidiaries were permitted to sell to China industrial parts purchased in the United States. Today there are virtually no restrictions on Americans traveling in China except those imposed by Peking. Washington has not suggested that these are anything but small steps, but they have not been reciprocated.

No one knows whether Peking would accept a seat in the United Nations if it were offered, but it seems evident that it would not do so unless (a) it were given China's seat on the Security Council, and (b) Taiwan were thrown out of the

[*] Ronald Steel, *Pax Americana* (New York: Viking, 1967), p. 132.

U. N. entirely. It is not clear why so many who consider it unethical to have mainland China excluded find it perfectly acceptable to exclude Taiwan, whose 13.3 million people make it one of the larger members of the U. N.

As for recognition, the Canadian experience shows how difficult it is to recognize Peking even when the decision has been made to do so. Negotiations between Canada and Communist China consumed two years because, although Canada was willing to acknowledge Peking as the "sole legal government" of China, it was unwilling to meet Peking's demand that this specifically include Taiwan.

Today, China and the Soviet Union have one thing in common above all else: a preoccupying fear that the other will form an alliance with the United States. Is it to be wondered that we feared the close alliance of these two monoliths and cannot even today quite rid ourselves of the anxiety that after the death of Mao they might restore their earlier relationship? Even now, the break seems in some ways inexplicable, especially as we were for so long assured by sympathetic students that ideology would overcome all differences. Though geopolitical and other factors suggested the possibility of a rupture, it could be pointed out that China desperately needed Soviet aid and that, with the United States a proclaimed enemy on its sea frontier, China could not afford another enemy on its vast land frontier. The pathology of a relatively weak nation which challenges the two most powerful nations on earth is interesting, but it does not lend assurance to the voice of those who tell us confidently what the Chinese will do or refrain from doing in Southeast Asia or elsewhere.

It is often said that we should not believe China and the Soviet Union when, in a variety of language, they say they will destroy us. We are assured that the bombastic things they say do not correspond to the relative caution of what they do. Such counsel may or may not be correct, but it is likely to fall on deaf ears. Many gave, and more heeded, the same advice regarding Hitler, only to find that *Mein Kampf* meant exactly what it said. Incredible as it seemed, as soon as Hitler believed he had the capacity, he set about fulfilling the letter of his forecasts. Hence it is not surprising that most Americans believe the leaders of China and the Soviet Union would carry out their verbal threats if they had the capability to do so, even at costs to themselves which we would find insupportable.* Mao's heir apparent, Lin Piao, has been both specific and faithful to his master's teaching: "It is opportunism [a particularly dirty word in the Communist lexicon] if one won't fight when one can win."

This is not a subject on which either side in the domestic debate can afford to be dogmatic, for all are dealing with the unknowable. Perhaps the experience with Nazi Germany is irrelevant, just as Pearl Harbor may have led us to believe erroneously that surprise attack is the most probable way another war might start. But who can be even tolerably sure?

For those who disbelieve what any American may say about the leading proponents of Communism, whom can we turn to as an authority with some credibility? Shall it be Karl Marx, who said of Russia: "Its methods, its tactics, its maneuvers may change, but the guiding star of this policy—world hegemony —will never change"? Or shall it be official statements of the Soviet Union accusing China of seeking total domination "if not of the whole world, then of Asia," and of causing the overthrow of Prince Sihanouk by its meddling in Cambodia's internal affairs? How about Mao as an authority? "The Soviet Union," he has said, officially, "is a dictatorship of the German fascist type, a dictatorship of the Hitler type." Few Western observers would go so far. Or this, from an editorial in an official Chinese publication:

* Those who find it outrageous to compare any of today's leaders with Hitler are generally those who did not live in the Hitler era. They do not recall his many apologists who pointed to the injustices done to Germany by the Versailles Treaty, just as historic injustices to Russia and China are used today to justify their behavior in the contemporary world.

Now the Soviet revisionist new czars have restored the old czars' policy of national oppression, adopted such cruel measures as discrimination, forced migration, splitting and imprisonment to oppress and persecute the minority nationalities and turned the Soviet Union back into the "prison of nations."

It vociferously preaches militarism, national chauvinism and racism and turns literature and art into tools for pushing social imperialism. In denouncing the dark rule of the czarist system, Lenin indicated that police tyranny, savage persecution and demoralization had reached such an extent that "the very stones cry out." One can just as well compare the rule of the Soviet revisionist renegade clique with the czarist system castigated by Lenin.

It talks glibly about practicing "internationalism" toward its so-called fraternal countries, but in fact it imposes fetter upon fetter, such as the "Warsaw Treaty Organization" and the "Council for Mutual Economic Assistance," on a number of East European countries and the Mongolian People's Republic, thereby confining them within its barbed-wire "socialist community" and freely ransacking them.

It has adopted the most despotic and vicious methods to keep these countries under strict control and stationed massive numbers of troops there, and it has even openly dispatched hundreds of thousands of troops to trample Czechoslovakia underfoot and install a puppet regime at bayonet point.

The Soviet revisionist renegade clique has taken over Khrushchev's military strategic principle of nuclear blackmail and energetically developed missile-nuclear weapons, and at the same time redoubled its efforts to expand conventional armaments, comprehensively strengthening its ground, naval and air forces, and carried out the imperialist "gunboat policy" throughout the world.

They have been increasing military expenditures still more frantically, stepping up their mobilization and preparation for wars of aggression and plotting to unleash a blitzkrieg of the Hitler type.*

* Excerpted in *The New York Times,* May 3, 1970.

Most of us do not respect Mao or his editorial writers as reliable sources of information or analysis and would prefer to use other authorities. Yet any Westerner who wrote even remotely in this vein would be excoriated as a Cold War monger by precisely those people who take Mao as a model of virtue to be emulated for his revolutionary zeal. Needless to say, the Russians do not share this impression. A few days after the foregoing editorial appeared, the Soviets responded with a Chinese-language broadcast which implied that Mao was the murderer of his first wife and son. The broadcast went on:

> Mao Tse-tung considers all the Chinese people a mass of inanimate objects—he may arbitrarily humiliate them, force them to suffer hardships or even let them die. Mao's cruelty and shamelessness can also be perceived from his statement that half of the Chinese population will die and the other half will continue to reproduce. He is unconcerned about the fate of his relatives or the multitudes.*

The United States, at least, has not stooped to this kind of name-calling. Our fear of Communism has been as nothing compared to our antagonists' fear of freedom. And our resistance to Communism has a positive side which critics ignore: For the new and weak nations it has kept options open, preserved alternatives. The contest between East and West has given the Third World a freedom they would not otherwise have enjoyed —a freedom to choose or postpone choice, to adopt elements of both systems or neither, to play each side off against the other and above all to avoid being locked into a system from which there is no escape. If we had thought only of our immediate defense and offered no resistance to Communism elsewhere in the world, this freedom of choice would have been foreclosed. This is not a justification of Vietnam, but the statement of a valid principle which in practice has obviously had

---

* *Ibid.*

negative as well as positive aspects and has led to mistakes as well as accomplishments.

Some of these issues will arise in later pages in other contexts. It is enough here to acknowledge that unquestionably American attitudes toward Communism have influenced policy, sometimes profoundly, occasionally irrationally and often inconsistently. It could hardly be otherwise. But this is quite different from asserting that anti-Communism has been the engine of all our acts or that exaggerated fears have wholly warped our judgment. For the first time in our history as a nation we have been learning to live with physical insecurity. If occasionally we seem to take a step back after two steps forward, our government has only reflected divisions and hesitancies in the American public, as well as the inconsistencies and thermal changes in the hostility of our antagonists.

IV

On Opposing Revolution
and Supporting Rightists

A GROUP of liberal intellectuals of an earlier generation spoke of revolution as "an obsessive myth of the modern mind in decay."* For today's liberal intellectual it appears to be a panacea, part of the natural disorder, a categorical imperative for breaking ancient patterns, for taking power from the few and giving it to the many. Our policy-makers have not been infected by this romanticism. Hence when it is said that the United States opposes revolution, it is generally true; it is also often irrelevant.

Revolutions occur against men and institutions, not against circumstances imposed by nature and the inescapable conditions of life. A state of revolt or the overturning of a government by force does not constitute a revolution. To have revolution, there must be something to tear down and ancient wrongs to right; there must be a rigid social and political structure highly resistant to change. The essence of revolution is radical change, and in most of the new nations old structures have already been torn down; in this sense the greater part of the world is already in a state of revolution.

When Chou En-lai went to Africa and announced that it

* Agar, *et al., The City of Man* (New York: Viking, 1940), p. 67.

was "ripe for revolution," he not only annoyed his hosts, most of whom considered themselves revolutionaries in having successfully won independence from the colonial powers, he simply misread the situation. Conditions for revolution do not exist in most of Africa. The exceptions are southern Africa, where the removal of white governments would constitute a genuine revolution; Ethiopia, which has a monarchy and a rigid hierarchical church; and possibly Morocco and Liberia. (Whether the overthrow of monarchy in Libya will amount to a revolution remains to be seen.) Elsewhere, all is in a state of flux; there are no established classes, no inherited wealth, no privileged groups except those holding political office. Revolts there are aplenty, and more will come. But revolution is impossible except in the sense that these states are already revolutionary. Regimes may seek to assert their independence of foreign economic influence by nationalizing industry and other measures; they may become more socialist or less so; or they may proclaim themselves Communist, as in the Congo (Brazzaville). They may kick against the pricks in a score of ways, none of which will constitute revolution, because they will not fundamentally alter conditions. For these newly independent states, radical change is already the order of the day, and if it is neither so radical nor so changing as they would wish, it is by reason of factors which revolution has not the capacity to change.

Latin America is a different story, but less so than many suppose. Bolivia had a genuine revolution in 1952—and the United States supported it. The tin mines, Bolivia's principal source of income, were nationalized; large landholdings were broken up and parcels distributed to the peasants. Otherwise little has changed. Bolivia is still the poorest country in South America, dependent upon the United States to make up budgetary deficits of between $15 million and $30 million a year. As before, governments come and go (187 in 139 years of independence). The military still wields the power, as it did before 1952, and the nation totters on the edge of civil war. The recent succession of leftist military governments and the nationalization of the Gulf Oil subsidiary in 1970 are unlikely to effect significant change in the country where Ché Guevara died in frustration and failure.

In the major countries of Latin America—Argentina, Brazil, Chile, Colombia and a few others—whether or not they are presently under military regimes, the obstacles to progress and distributive justice are not primarily the power of small oligarchies or the dominance of landed aristocracies. Power is much more diffuse than is generally supposed. Substantial entrepreneurial and intellectual classes have interests which by no means conform to that of the landed aristocracy, and the leadership groups of greatest influence are for the most part only one or two generations removed from the peasantry or are sons or grandsons of European immigrants.

Paradoxically, the presence of a military regime in Argentina today is due more to the strength of the labor unions than to their weakness. In Brazil, where the military has traditionally stayed out of politics, the present junta came on the heels of a leftist, possibly revolutionary, regime, which had brought the country annual inflation of more than 130 percent. All groups now suffer political oppression, but the present regime is doing more to develop Brazil economically than all its predecessors. If the junta is thrown out, it will probably be by those who thought they would be well served by a military regime and were not—namely, the middle and entrepreneurial classes—or by a group of younger officers. Each country shows its own peculiarities. In Peru, for example, which does have some revolutionary potential, a relatively progressive and democratic government was overthrown by a military regime which professes to be leftist and revolutionary; this remains to be seen. In Chile, where only 1.27 percent of the registered voters are members of the Communist Party, the electorate recently turned out of office the most progressive regime in the country's history and replaced it with a Marxist government pledged to uphold the existing constitution.

To the extent that generalities have any validity for all of Latin America, it can be said that the failure to accomplish what is politically and socially necessary is due less to the power of selfish oligarchies than to a combination of other factors: the lack of continuity of government; the prevalence of corrupt and demogogic leaders who may be replaced, but not with assurance of change; the intense partisanship which makes politicians less interested in getting things done than in getting credit for them (an ill not confined to Latin America, but excessive there); the consequent difficulty of building consensuses; the aspirations of the rising middle class for social recognition rather than political power. These factors and others, some of which are less within the leaders' control—such as unfavorable terms of trade and limited domestic markets—may seem to be a prescription for revolution, but they are not likely to be altered by it.

Asia is again somewhat different. There, old established societies may be vulnerable to revolts which could assume the proportions of revolution, but it does not seem likely. Apart from South Vietnam, and Laos and Cambodia, which are assailed from outside as well as within, the most susceptible at present is the Philippines, a country with the forms but not the substance of democracy, resistant to change and mired in corruption and violence. Elsewhere, revolution is conceivable, but would probably take the form of civil war among ethnic and religious groups (India, Indonesia, Malaysia) or would, by the nature of the indigenous problems, be unlikely to effect more radical change than is already in progress.

Passing over Eastern Europe, which has been, and may still be, the most concentrated area of revolutionary potential, let us assume, then, that there are perhaps a dozen nations in the world where conditions for revolution exist and where revolution might in time bring beneficial change. Setting aside the cost in blood, which revolutionaries are by definition prepared to pay, is revolution really a shortcut to a more just society? The historical evidence suggests otherwise. Most "successful" revolutions have simply transferred power from one oligarchy to another. Where revolutions have effected profound changes, as in France, Russia and perhaps Mexico, they have been accompanied by protracted civil war, and destruction not merely of the power structure but the very fabric of society. Those who instituted the revolution rarely retained control, and recovery from the ensuing chaos required decades. The Chinese Revolution is instructive in this regard. Mao retained control of the revolution initially, then blew his considerable achievement eighteen years later. The Cultural Revolution not only destroyed the party and set back the economy and education three years; it transferred power to the Army, where it primarily resides today, and it re-created a degree of regional autonomy, which has been the weakness of China for centuries.

In the Russian Revolution, not less than seven million were killed or died in concentration camps, most of them in the second decade after the revolution. In China death was inflicted on more than a million in the first phase of the revolution, though how many more we may never know; the Cultural Revolution brought another round of death and sheer destruction of the lives of millions of the living. In North Vietnam at least 100,000 were killed and some 900,000 fled to the south before Ho Chi Minh had gained total control. In each instance, those who died were not predominantly exploiters or enemies of the people but small farmers and respected village chiefs. For Americans to go about indiscriminately promoting revolution is trifling with human life on a very large scale; it is also to encourage intervention in the affairs of other nations of a more fundamental kind than the U. S. government has ever had the arrogance to essay.

Who, after all, is to say what countries need revolution and what form it should take? The Chinese have urged the Soviet populace to launch a "people's revolution" against Moscow's "fascist dictatorship" maintained with "tanks and armored cars" and the use of "special agents and spies." Who will agree that Russia needs another revolution? Besides Mao, the extreme rightists will. Most others, even those who most passionately hope that Russia may one day achieve democracy, would feel that further revolution there would serve no one's interest—not the Russian people's, not ours, not democracy's.

The notion that revolution is the fast way to effect change, and evolution the slow way, is not borne out by an examination of history. Thus it is doubtful that nations which are most urgently in need of the alleged benefits of revolution can afford the time, even if the goals could be achieved. Also, it is these same countries in which the requisite organizational ability is lacking; they may be capable of anarchy, but not of revolution. A further consideration is that the price of revolution would seem unnecessarily high today. Those few countries which are politically ossified are islands in an already revolutionary world. This lends substance to the hope that by a process of contagion change can be brought about by less violent means.

However this may be, it will be useful to examine our most intimate experience with revolution in the postwar period, for it demonstrates that we have by no means been anti-revolutionary. Between those who have willfully forgotten and those who never knew of the United States' early reaction to the Cuban revolution, the story has been very seriously distorted.

That we helped to create revolution in Cuba is undoubtedly true, first by our inexcusable toleration of the dictator Batista (though Castro later acknowledged that Batista had been skillful in obscuring his oppression), then by helping Castro in a variety of small ways. Castro obtained his first unofficial aid in the United States several years before the revolution. He was almost unheard of until *The New York Times* extensively reported his activities in the Sierra Maestra, painting him as a romantic figure and the hope of Cuba. Then belatedly Wash-

ington cut off arms aid to Batista and turned its back on him—
circumstances which had much to do with Castro's success.
The first country that Castro visited after he attained power on
January 1, 1959, was the United States, where he was given
a hero's welcome.

In Washington, New York and Boston, he was greeted by
tumultuous crowds. President Eisenhower was vacationing in
Georgia and Secretary of State Dulles was mortally ill in the
hospital, but Castro lunched with Acting Secretary Herter, met
with the Senate Foreign Relations Committee and the House
Foreign Affairs Committee and spent two and a half hours
with Vice-President Nixon, reporting afterward that the con-
versation had been "friendly, informal and positive." As he
left Washington, he was asked whether he had achieved what
he had hoped for. "Yes," he replied, nodding vigorously, "I
really believe."

That evening in Princeton, he was greeted by more than a
thousand cheering students and delivered a lecture. He was
the house guest of Governor Robert B. Meyner and there met
former Secretary of State Dean Acheson. Arriving in New
York by train next morning, he was met by twenty-thousand
people, all but a handful of whom were wildly enthusiastic.
Everywhere he went in New York—to City Hall to be greeted
by the mayor, to Columbia University or to a rally on the
Central Park mall—there were crowds pressing to see him and
to shake his hand. Two of his comments as reported by *The
New York Times* are significant. After receiving the keys of
the city at ceremonies on the mall, Castro said, "The rich nation of the north has understood our just cause, and that understanding of our desires constitutes the real triumph." And
speaking at the Overseas Press Club, he said he would return
to Cuba with "a stronger faith" in the bond of friendship between his country and the United States. Then he added in
his unreliable English, "I think you will never be repented
of the honor you give us."

During his first visit, Castro also appeared on "Meet the

Press" and spoke before the American Society of Newspaper Editors, the National Press Club, the foreign correspondents of the United Nations, the Women Lawyers' Association of the State of New York and that alleged epicenter of the American Establishment, the Council on Foreign Relations. It is doubtful that any "unofficial" visitor to the United States ever received a warmer welcome, addressed more important and influential groups or was so exhaustively covered by press and television. As a government and as a people, we belied the notion that we are anti-revolutionary.

In all of his speeches during his visit, Castro emphasized a few points: (1) he had come to the United States not to ask for money but for "sympathy and understanding"; (2) his "heart lay with the democracies," he "did not agree with Communism" and did not intend to be neutral; (3) he favored nonintervention—"The Cuban Revolution is not for export"; (4) the trials by military tribunals would soon be over and in many cases appeal to civilian courts would be permitted; (5) Cuba would not confiscate foreign private property—indeed, more foreign investment was desired.

At the time, there was some skepticism about each of these points. Indeed, even while Castro was visiting the United States, a group of Cubans was landing in Panama in an effort to provoke a revolution, though it is not clear whether Castro knew of it. But before the end of the year (Castro's visit was in April) there could not be any doubt that each of Castro's points was false. Moreover, by then he not only was trying "to export the Cuban revolution" to rightist dictatorships in the Caribbean, but was landing guerrillas in Venezuela, which had an unquestionably democratic government. Even after extended vilification of the United States, expropriation of more than a billion dollars of American investment, and arrest and expulsion of American citizens, the United States was slow to retaliate. "By any normal standards, the self-restraint displayed by the United States through many months of Cuban harassment would have been remarkable even had the Cuban situation seemed unrelated to the global offensive of international Communism."* It was not until mid-1960 that all economic aid was cut off and the sugar quota reduced to an inconsequential level.

Castro insisted on having the United States as an enemy. Much as today's New Left does not want compromise but total confrontation, so Castro demanded U. S. hostility. In the spring of 1959, Castro could have got almost anything he wanted from us. Feeling guilty for our previous support of Batista and conscious of Castro's popularity throughout the hemisphere, not to mention the genuinely sympathetic response to him by a majority of Americans, we had no motive and no disposition to do him in. It was even understood that Castro needed to make us his whipping boy and we were prepared to accept a good deal of abuse, however inconsistent with his earlier attitudes. As it was, he made Washington's position politically impossible.

Whether Castro calculated that any compromise whatever with the United States would have weakened his role in Latin America or whether he was even then a true-believing Communist we do not know. The evidence weighs toward the former explanation. In any event, by avowing Communism and making Cuba even more dependent on the Soviet Union than it had formerly been on the United States, he managed to reduce his stature and effectiveness in Latin America, lower the standard of living in his country and rekindle in Americans a fear of Communism that had begun to subside. Clearly the experience did not make it easier for policy-makers to deal with other revolutionaries in subsequent years.

It does not help, either, that the great bulk of intellectuals appear to see in revolution a good in and of itself. A maverick among them, Irving Kristol has asked:

* Richard P. Stebbins, *The United States in World Affairs, 1960* (New York: Harper, for the Council on Foreign Relations, 1961), p. 303.

Is it conceivable that American intellectuals should *ever* disapprove of *any* popular revolution, anywhere in the world—whatever the express or implicit principles of this revolution? One can make this question even sharper: Is it conceivable for American intellectuals ever to approve of their government suppressing, or helping to frustrate, any popular revolution by *poor people*—whatever the nature or consequences of this revolution? The answer would obviously have to be in the negative; and the implications of this answer for American foreign policy are not insignificant. This policy must work within a climate of opinion that finds the idea of a *gradual* evolution of traditional societies thoroughly uninteresting—which, indeed, has an instinctive detestation of all traditional societies as being inherently unjust, and an equally instinctive approval, as being inherently righteous, of any revolutionary ideology which claims to incorporate the people's will.*

Thus many of those who accuse the United States of "indiscriminately" supporting rightist regimes and opposing revolution are in fact wholly undiscriminating themselves. Furthermore, in urging revolution hither and yon they take upon themselves a heavy responsibility of the sort they deplore in their government.

More charitably, perhaps it is because the word "revolution" has come to be used so loosely in other contexts—rising expectations, morals, communications, etc.—that so many people feel they ought to be in favor of it. Or perhaps it is because we pride ourselves on "our" Revolution and believe others deserve no less. Historians are in dispute as to whether we had a revolution in the eighteenth century. What we did have was a war for independence followed by the most imaginative and constructive political experimentation ever compressed into one generation; it was conducted by the established leadership of the society, excluding those who were unreconciled to separation from Britain or had served her too well. Radical

* Irving Kristol, "American Intellectuals and Foreign Policy," *Foreign Affairs,* July 1967, p. 599.

change there was indeed, but as the term is being used today it was not a revolution. Our own happy experience with radical change at the time of our nation's birth should not obscure the fact that political revolutions are profoundly destructive for periods not of months but of years, and whether they can then become constructive is problematical.

And so, not without reason, we emphasize evolution, though this need not imply either excessive gradualism or the illusion that instability can thereby be avoided. It is true that we are predisposed to order and stability, for a modicum of both is necessary for free choice and rational decision. We are wary of those who may exploit instability, including rogues and opportunists who may have no commitment to Communism. But no one in government supposes that change, which is seen as necessary, can occur without some instability, or that political and economic development can occur with an excess of it.

The sweeping generalization that the United States supports authoritarian governments misses the point. First, there are probably as many authoritarian governments of the left as of the right. It is not a self-evident rule that those of the left are preferable. Second, in Latin America, where we exert greater influence than elsewhere and where the cycle of coups and countercoups has been most prolonged, we have, with a very few exceptions, cut off aid to any country where a constitutionally elected government was replaced by other than constitutional means. Where we have resumed support, we have done so reluctantly and in the conviction that by withholding aid we were hurting the people, not the regime (see Chapter VIII). Our alleged support of rightist military governments has been equivocal at best, while our support for democratically elected governments has been far more substantial.

In Africa, we vigorously opposed the regime of Moïse Tshombe in Katanga despite enormous pressure from some of our allies and from a powerful lobby in the United States which insisted that Mr. Tshombe was the only reliable anti-Communist in the Congo (see Chapter V).

Recently Greece has been offered as Exhibit A to support the contention that we support rightist military regimes. Insinuations that the United States connived in the overthrow of the legitimate government of Greece in April 1967 have been followed by charges that we have been instrumental in keeping the junta in power. There is not a shred of evidence for the first accusation, and the second is pure hypothesis; but even after seven years in Vietnam, the illusion lingers—and especially among Greeks—that the United States can do anything it wills. It is ironic that the exiled leaders of a country which "in the last 50 years alone has suffered two civil wars, eight military coups d'etat and a change of government on the average nearly once a year"* should have to find a scapegoat for the latest round of folly and cruelty. Even the regime's much-publicized political prisoners—now numbering about five hundred—are fewer than the norm for Greece over the last forty years.

The United States decided in the early sixties that it should gradually lessen its involvement in Greek affairs, which had been substantial after Britain withdrew as protector and benefactor in 1947. Greeks who opposed a less active American role, as well as those who applauded it, doubted that we meant it and continued—as they do today—to exaggerate our capacity and willingness to shape events. When the coup came, we were taken as unawares as were the King and his ministers. The King deplored the takeover, but nevertheless agreed to swear in the generals, thereby giving them a measure of legitimacy. Thereafter we did no less and slightly more than any other government to show our disapproval of the new regime. No foreign government withdrew recognition. The United States alone did more than express its dissatisfaction with

* David Holden, chief foreign correspondent of the London *Sunday Times,* writing in *The New York Times Book Review,* May 31, 1970.

words: it cut off all major military aid. Other than that, we had very little leverage beyond power of persuasion, especially as in the early stages the regime had considerable popularity. Particularly in the countryside, which is profoundly conservative, people were fed up with the noisy bickering of Greece's politicians and the uncertainties of everyday life. Publicly and privately, however, we urged the junta to set a date for the restoration of democratic government, pointing out that after the military coup in Turkey in 1960, power had been returned to the civilians within eighteen months, and that Greeks certainly could do no less.

A series of events then occurred which almost unavoidably lessened our capacity to exert pressure on the junta. Six weeks after the coup in Athens the Six-Day War broke out in the Middle East. Thousands of Americans and others were evacuated, and almost all had to be taken out through Athens as the nearest available relay point. The junta turned itself inside out to be helpful. Turkey, wishing to avoid involvement, indicated that its NATO facilities could be used only against the enemies of NATO. Thus the bases and harbors of Greece were the easternmost installations available in a highly unpredictable situation. Though the swiftness of the Israeli victory made them unnecessary, the Greek regime used the brief time effectively to ingratiate itself with the United States. This is not to say the junta won any concessions, but its cooperation undoubtedly made it harder for the United States to show its hostility.

Next came the flare-up over Cyprus in which two of our NATO allies came within a hair's breadth of war. The Turks were poised for attack when the U. S. President dispatched a special emissary (Cyrus Vance) in a last-ditch effort to find a solution. The good offices of a skillful and tireless diplomat flying among the three capitals would not be enough. Nor would maximum pressure by the United States, although this was used. What ultimately saved the situation was that Greece's military regime, counseled by a shrewd civilian Foreign Minister, agreed to withdraw Greek troops from Cyprus. It was a decision that no civilian government of recent memory in Athens would have had the will or the political strength to make. Again, we were put in the awkward position of being grateful to a regime we abhorred.

The third circumstance within hardly more than a year was the Soviet invasion of Czechoslovakia. Europe was not only appalled at the destruction of liberalism in Prague but alarmed by the shift in the balance of forces created by the movement of Soviet troops hundreds of miles farther westward. Even Yugoslavia, which itself was preparing for a possible Soviet invasion, wanted nothing so much as stability in Greece. At the same time, Russian naval forces in the Mediterranean were mounting steadily, with the result that NATO's port facilities seemed increasingly essential not merely to the Americans but to the Alliance as a whole.

The times, then, were hardly propitious for bringing maximum pressure on the junta, and it is difficult to see how our interests would have been served by doing so. There is no evidence to suggest that it would have dislodged the regime. To be sure, we should as a matter of principle have stopped delivery of *all* arms, though our cutoff of major military equipment had no visible effect on the junta except to induce some cynical gestures toward Moscow. Also, we were careless in allowing American officers in NATO to be used by the regime to give the appearance of support. The routine visit of an American aircraft carrier should have been canceled, and U. S. officers should be more skillful in avoiding being photographed with members of the junta. But as long as Greece is in NATO—and none of the Greek political factions except the Communists wants it thrown out—periodic visits by NATO brass are routine and inescapable, though the number has been greatly reduced.

Greek politicians are charter members of that vast tribe around the world who seek American intervention when it serves their purposes and complain the rest of the time about

American interference. Some have built their careers on anti-Americanism, have shown their devotion to Greece by voluntarily spending years abroad, and have themselves been implicated in efforts—just before the coup—to overthrow the government. None can escape responsibility for the anguish his country is now suffering. To accuse the United States, without substantiation, of abetting the enemies of democracy, which has never established itself in Greece, comes with a particularly bad grace from politicians who themselves have done so little to promote it.

This is not to condone Greece's military regime, which is patently oppressive and incompetent. The experience does illustrate two points: first, critics at home and abroad apply a double standard, welcoming U. S. interference when it serves their political predilections, opposing it when it does not; and, second, any simple principle that we shall not tolerate right-wing dictatorships can be made excruciatingly difficult in particular circumstances. The most dangerous situation in the world today is not in Southeast Asia but in the Middle East. To expect the United States to do anything which might weaken the southern flank of NATO at a time when the Russians are appearing there in ever greater numbers as technicians, sailors and fighter pilots is to invite irresponsibility. Even the most dovish members of the Senate have spoken out in favor of a firm policy against the "ominous and provocative" actions of the Soviet Union in the Middle East.

Critics who would forbid us to have relations with rightist military dictatorships often encourage close relations with those that lean to the left. They are entitled to their preference, but they cannot exercise it under the banner of democracy, or even of revolution. When U. S. policy-makers err in their judgments, they are not permitted to forget it. But how many recall the fervor with which our government some years ago was urged to support President Kwame Nkrumah of Ghana as the wave of the future, leader of the "radical" African states, true fighter against neocolonialism and for the unification of Africa? His advocates chose to ignore the mounting evidence that Nkrumah was a vain and grasping despot who was oppressing his own people and grievously dividing black Africa. Our increasing reluctance to maintain cordial relations with him, as had been the case earlier, or to support him in his international adventures, was explained by many as simply due to Nkrumah's "pro-Communist" sympathies. Little credence was given to the more substantial causes of our discontent: that he was wasting Ghana's resources in monuments to his own ego, that he had obliterated freedom in Ghana and filled its prisons with his political opponents, and that he was trying to subvert neighboring governments in the hope of establishing regimes more to his liking. Subsequently, of course, Nkrumah was overthrown and democracy reestablished. Unlike some dictators who have been toppled, he appears to be in total disgrace in the eyes of his countrymen and of most Africans. Our refusal to support Nkrumah to the end served us in good stead. The wonder is that so many would have had us support him simply because he was reputed to be radical and leftist, without regard for other qualities.

A quite different case is that of Peru, now under a leftist military dictatorship which overthrew a constitutionally elected, relatively progressive government. Despite reservations about some of the regime's policies, such as serious infringement of press freedom, we have maintained friendly relations —in part, at least, because the junta seems purposeful and dedicated. Even before the disastrous earthquake in the spring of 1970, we were extending economic aid and continuing Peru's sugar quota. Moreover, we were doing this in defiance of the law.* This involved virtually a conspiracy of silence by

---

* The Hickenlooper amendment to the Foreign Assistance Act requires the suspension of aid to a country which expropriates American property and makes no move over a period of six months to provide fair compensation. In October 1968, the Peruvian government nationalized without compensation American oil and refinery properties officially appraised at $71 million.

Congressmen and others. Can one imagine such a silence if the United States aided Greece with bland disregard for an act of Congress? This is not to say we should have cut off aid to Peru. The Hickenlooper amendment is a bad law and ought to be repealed.

Our experience and relations with authoritarian regimes suggests that our policies have been formulated out of complex causes—not out of any simplistic notion that radical is risky and conservative is safe. In international affairs, certainly no less than in other spheres, preferred conduct and the principles one professes are not easy to adhere to in all circumstances. Even if the making of decisions were not a complicated process of pull and haul, of weighing unattractive alternatives, of reaching compromises, our policies and actions would not be blessed with perfect consistency. It is odd that those who find fault with inconsistency in so many aspects of policy should accuse their country of consistently opposing revolution and supporting rightist dictatorships. The record is otherwise.

V

Overcommitment and
Intervention

We come now to the heart of the matter, for it is here that a wide variety of critics meet on shared ground: the United States is overcommitted, they say, in that we have neither the strength nor the warrant for being the world's policeman; and, not unrelated to this, we are led (or choose) to intervene in the affairs of other nations without justification.

It will not be the purpose of this chapter to disprove these contentions, but to try to put them in better perspective and remind ourselves that in international affairs there are few absolutes. Certainly, though, after twenty years of rapid change and a mixed bag of experience in which the tragedy of Vietnam weighs most heavily, we do indeed need to reexamine our commitments and try to sharpen our perception of the circumstances in which intervention, especially military intervention, may—if ever—be justified.

Let us start with some questions:

What is intervention? Should it be defined only in military terms? Most people would agree that "dirty tricks" by the CIA are intervention, but what about arming one side against the other in a dispute? Or becoming involved in a U. N. peacekeeping operation (as in the Congo), where the conflict may have Cold War implications? Or using every arm-twisting device available to a superpower to deter two allies from going to war with each other (as we did on two occasions with Greece and Turkey)? Can we tolerate other Communist regimes in the Caribbean and, if so, how many? Are we intervening in Europe by virtue of our participation in NATO? Are we intervening in the domestic affairs of another nation when we set conditions for foreign aid—even minimal economic conditions essential to development?

Is there a distinction to be made between legal and illegal interventions? Are we justified in intervening in Berlin, where we have legal rights, but unjustified in intervening in, say, South Africa, where we do not? Or is there a moral imperative that is above law? Two hundred million Africans want us to intervene in southern Africa to end white racism; should this affect our decision? Does it make a difference if we intervene at the request of a constitutional government? The United Nations considers this difference essential with regard to its own interventions, but when we set the same condition, we are accused of having contrived the invitation.

With the threat but without the necessity of force, we intervened in 1956 on behalf of Egypt and against our allies—not primarily, as some assert, because we were afraid of the Soviet Union, but because we considered Britain and France guilty of naked aggression. Was this unjustified? Should we do less for Israel if she finds herself in a similar position?

If we could define aggression, perhaps we could resolve to intervene militarily only where aggression was demonstrable. But experts cannot agree on what constitutes aggression, and the United Nations labored for a decade to agree on a definition, but without success. This is hardly surprising in view of the dispute within the United States as to whether North Vietnam has committed aggression against South Vietnam—or indeed whether the United States was the aggressor in Southeast Asia. All we can be reasonably sure of is that overt military forces marching across international boundaries will be less likely than in the past. Shall we agree that we are not concerned with subversion even if there is outside help? Or only sometimes, somewhere?

Richard Rovere, a rigorous critic of American foreign policy and an early opponent of the war in Vietnam, has written:

> Most future wars are apt to be like the war in Vietnam—wars that will be called by instigators "wars of liberation." The Soviet Union, as Nikita Khrushchev long ago informed us, will support them. From its point of view, they are irresistible. They cost next to nothing and drive us Americans out of our minds. But if we survive as anything like a free society, we will not be entering them. I simply cannot imagine this country, under any President chosen in a free election, taking on another Vietnam. If this is so, it may be good news. But it means that we won't have much in the way of a foreign policy. We will draw back from all difficult situations. We will leave the field to those who have not renounced war.*

The question that Rovere does not answer is whether we can remain a free society *and* leave the field to those who have not renounced war. The answer is not self-evident.

John W. Holmes, of the Canadian Institute of International Affairs and a frequent, though friendly critic of the United States, has made the point more sharply:

> In their dismay over this wretched [Vietnam] war, Canadians, Europeans and many Americans are losing their sense of proportion, ignoring the indispensability of American power and productivity in any calculations for a happier world. . . . We are particularly conscious at present of the danger of the United States jumping too quickly into intervention. We must not forget, however, that the Communists' doctrine of supporting whatever they choose to nominate as "wars of liberation" remains a serious threat to UN authority. They should not be encouraged by an abdication of resistance. No great

* *The New Yorker,* Oct. 28, 1968, pp. 84-85.

power should be allowed to pursue its aims in the world without resistance. If we have reached a more hopeful stage in relations between East and West, this has come out of confrontation, not by the abandonment of resistance. This is a time to think about reciprocal, not unilateral, dismantling of the military structures which have brought us not peace or certainty but more hope of continuing security than we have had for centuries.*

One of the questions we shall have to answer is: Are we living in One World or are we not? Thirty years ago liberals generally agreed that the answer was affirmative. Now, after an intervening revolution in transportation and communication which has shrunk the world to a fraction of its then size, there are doubters saying that, while military intervention in Europe or Latin America may be justified in extreme circumstances, it can never be justified in Asia or Africa. Our interests, it is said, do not require it, and our power does not allow it. (Others feel that intervention is justified in South Africa but not in the Dominican Republic.) But, as Albert Wohlstetter has recently shown, neither our interests nor our power can be measured in lineal distance.† Modern transport and communication has made distance inconsequential. In Vietnam the logistical problem has not been to get men and supplies to the mouth of the Saigon River, but to get them from there to where they were needed. A recent study indicates that if Korea had been two-thousand miles farther away, the added cost of the war would have been three tenths of one percent. On the Thai–Laos border the United States can lift, from 8,500 miles away, four times as much as China can from 450 miles away. But, what is more important, our interests—even our knowledge—do not necessarily decline with distance. Our interest in the Middle East is comparable to our interest in the Caribbean;

* Address at Victoria College, Toronto, Jan. 30, 1968 (mimeographed).
† Albert Wohlstetter, "Illusions of Distance," *Foreign Affairs,* January 1968.

we certainly know more about India than about most of the countries of Latin America, and our concerns are as great. We can hardly be indifferent to what happens to 550 million Indians. This is not to argue that all our involvements in Asia are justified, but to point out that distance is no longer a criterion of our interests or capabilities.

Before World War II, the United States was a great power among many great powers; we emerged from that war a superpower. The difference is that we now have less freedom of action (or inaction), not more. For today what we refrain from doing may be as significant and as consequential as what we do. As Irving Kristol has pointed out, it is not anyone's decision or overweaning ambition that has caused us to have special responsibilities, but the nature of the world and the preponderance of our power. Our choices are more limited than some would have us believe.

For example, the choice of becoming a regional power, as we were in the last century, is simply not available to us. Some of the reasons have been noted; they have only partly to do with the threats to our interests and security presented by the Soviet Union and China. Of growing and perhaps greater significance in the long run is the simple fact that the interests of mankind are now so fundamentally interlocked.

> In the past, differences were "livable" because of time and distance that separated them. Today, these differences are actually widening while technetronics are eliminating the two insulants of time and distance. The resulting trauma could create almost entirely different perspectives on life, with insecurity, envy, and hostility becoming the dominant emotions for increasingly large numbers of people.*

From this there will be no escape into a Fortress America any more than a rich man can lock himself in a mansion and ignore the problems of his community. Some have seen an es-

* Zbigniew Brzezinski in *Encounter,* December 1967, p. 25.

cape from responsibility in the growth of regional centers of power and an apparent increase in multipolarity. But the prospects are not bright. Physical proximity does not necessarily make for closeness; more often it heightens fears. The most ancient and bitter antagonisms are generally between close neighbors. Even where there are no specific territorial or other disputes, there are fears among small nations of domination by large ones. And large ones close at hand appear more menacing than those at a distance. When President de Gaulle was seeking to break what he considered to be American hegemony in Europe, some Europeans were disturbed, others delighted, but not one wanted to substitute French protection for American.

Robert Osgood has observed:

Historically, it is remarkable that, twenty years after a major war causing a decisive redistribution of power, the immediate postwar configurations of power and alignment among the major powers should not have changed more fundamentally. Within twenty years after other such wars in modern times, the structure of power has been upset or radically challenged; the issues of conflict, the pattern of alignments, and the major contestants have changed.*

Another option that is not open to us is to remove commitments where in fact we believe we have vital interests—though in some cases the commitment could be made more limited. For example, the weight of evidence is that if we had not indicated that Korea was excluded from our defense perimeter, there would have been no war there. That is, the North Koreans would not have attacked if they had known we would resist. Once they had attacked, it was apparent—apart from other considerations—that the threat posed to Japan was unacceptable; it had to be opposed. Hence it is not true to say that commitments invariably lead to military involvements; they may also prevent them.

* Osgood, Tucker and others, *America and the World from the Truman Doctrine to Vietnam* (Baltimore and London: Johns Hopkins, 1970), p. 15.

Unless we can reduce our commitments very substantially, we must also face the fact that it will be difficult to reduce our conventional forces below what will still seem to be a high level. Just as there is nothing more dangerous than sending an inadequate police force to quell a riot, so force in the international scene must be adequate to the responsibilities that have been assumed or acquired by default. In a "police action" or in an intervention designed to prevent a war or to separate belligerents, force is a means of avoiding violence, and that is why, in the Dominican Republic and Lebanon, we sent forces far larger than appeared to be needed.

Some will ask why we cannot abjure such labors entirely and rely on the United Nations. This, of course, was the role foreseen for the U. N. when it was created, but effectiveness depended on the major powers—the permanent members of the Security Council—pulling together. And this ended very quickly with the beginnings of the Cold War. Nevertheless, for a number of years the U. N. achieved some successes in coping with tough political issues and in mounting peace-keeping operations. This was accomplished by giving the General Assembly a larger role and placing faith in a strong and imaginative Secretary General. Armed with extensive but intentionally vague instructions, Dag Hammarskjöld could interpret his authority as broadly as the active support of at least some of the major powers and the acquiescence of others permitted. This was essentially the basis on which the Congo operation was conducted—the most ambitious undertaking ever essayed by the U. N. and virtually its last effort of consequence in the political-security field. The absence of vigorous leadership by Mr. Hammarskjöld's successor combined with the growing caution and cynicism of a majority of members means that the U. N. not only does not seek a major role, it conspires to avoid it. To be sure, the U. N. is only the sum of its parts and must depend on the cooperation and support of the major powers. But instead of cultivating that cooperation and support, the members have frittered away what influence they had on what are too often parochial and irrelevant concerns. Most notably the U. N. has avoided any involvement in Southeast Asia on the grounds that, where the superpowers are involved, nothing can be risked. The United Nations is still capable of accomplishment, but not, apparently, in keeping the peace or settling disputes. The organization is being used by its members rather than being made useful. Almost everyone has lost confidence in the U. N., including the United States. But this does not mean that we have been unwilling to submit issues to it (though our record here has not been consistent). Rather, it is the U. N. which has been unwilling to deal with issues in which the United States or the Soviet Union are involved. As the U. N. has no peace-keeping forces of its own and its members seem increasingly reluctant to provide them, the world organization does not at present offer an alternative means of keeping the peace or preventing aggression.

Let us now look very briefly at several instances of American intervention, starting from the premise that most of them are difficult to justify and that we must make every effort in the future to avoid them. Nevertheless, even the worst instances are not quite so reprehensible as they have been painted, and some have served a useful purpose.*

THE DOMINICAN REPUBLIC.   The weight of evidence is that our military intervention in the spring of 1965 was unjustified —certainly in law and probably in terms of national security. Washington appears to have overreacted on the basis of inadequate or distorted information, and it certainly acted with unnecessary haste. The failure to consult the Organization of American States was destructive of policy and principle. But to paint the landing of the Marines as a vicious act of aggres-

---

* It may reasonably be pointed out that in the period under review we intervened in Germany and Japan with some success. No one today questions that it was warranted or that we did rather well in putting two totalitarian militaristic nations on a different course, winning their respect in the process.

sion, as some American critics have done, is to abandon all sense of proportion.

For over a century rebellion and civil war have been endemic to the Dominican Republic; tyranny and torture have been the norm. The last to rule by terror was Trujillo, who was assassinated in 1961, a year after the United States, much too tardily, had broken diplomatic relations. For the next four years, amidst disruptive factionalism, we made a strenuous and generally impartial effort to encourage political agreement and economic development. When yet another military coup appeared in the making, the American President sent eight ships with 1,800 Marines to cruise offshore; the coup was deterred. When Juan Bosch became the constitutionally elected President by a comfortable majority in 1962, he was, on the authority of Senator Fulbright, "warmly and repeatedly embraced and supported as few if any Latin American Presidents have ever been supported by the United States." Though he was distinctly on the left, he was granted aid in the amount of $84 million in an eighteen-month period and was saved by the United States from one coup. But in less than two years he had, by his own incompetence, antagonized every element of the population, and his government fell. The United States immediately cut off all military and economic aid.

Nineteen months later, on April 24, 1965, a rebellion broke out.* Each of the parties in the three-way struggle—the fallen government of Donald Reid Cabral, the "old" military types, and a group of rebels representing many factions but rallying under the banner of the absent Bosch—all bid aggressively for American support. Perhaps mistakenly, none was helped in the intervening days until the Marines landed early in May.

* Senator Fulbright, in *The Arrogance of Power* (New York: Random House, 1967, p. 86), calls it a "Revolution" with a capital *R*, apparently to demonstrate that the United States opposes revolution. Unless one is prepared to say that the rebels were indeed controlled by Castro Communists, which the Senator is not, there is absolutely no warrant for calling the umpteenth overthrow of a Dominican government a revolution.

Though it may well be true that their primary mission was not to protect American lives, as Washington contended, the fact remains that, with public order deteriorating day by day, Dominican and American lives were undoubtedly saved. Although it is said that during the occupation we acted in the interests of the conservatives, the only notable leader ejected from the country on American authority was the rightist leader, General Wessin y Wessin. Within five months U. S. troops were withdrawn and within fourteen months a democratically elected government was again in power. Many of the old vices of Dominican politics have since returned—authoritarianism, corruption and unimaginative leadership among them. Still out of power, Mr. Bosch now says that the country's problems can be solved only by dictatorship.

Whether there was warrant for fearing that the rebels were dominated by Communists or that the rebellion would be taken over by Communists—or whether it mattered—it cannot be gainsaid that from a domestic political viewpoint, "another Cuba" off our shores would have been a disaster. One does not have to agree with the President's decision to feel some sympathy for the Administration's dilemma.

To compare our actions in the Dominican Republic with those of the Soviet Union in Czechoslovakia is natural but invalid. We did not frustrate the will of the people; there was not then and is not now a clear mandate for anything in the Dominican Republic—certainly not for Communism. We intervened between warring factions in a rebellion led initially by military officers allied with the followers of Juan Bosch. Having restored a measure of order, we encouraged free elections, in which Bosch was badly beaten. Nevertheless, the landing of U. S. forces was an illegal act and an instance of intervention which might have been avoided.

LEBANON. In the early summer of 1958, the Lebanese government appealed to the United States to intervene to prevent what it claimed was external subversion. Lebanon is a fragile society which has survived by a conscious effort to maintain a balance of powers, privileges and official posts between its Christian and Muslim communities. It has also sought to stay out of the political squabbles of the area. As of that time, Lebanon had established itself after fifteen years of independence as the most stable and democratic of the Arab countries.

In 1958 a number of factors conspired to place this state of affairs in jeopardy. Arab nationalism was arousing passions among Lebanon's Muslims, and the formation of the United Arab Republic (composed of Egypt and Syria) was whetting hopes for Arab unity. The Lebanese government of President Camille Chamoun was taking a strongly pro-American position, while its Arab neighbors were turning increasingly to the Soviet Union for arms and aid. Growing tensions in Lebanon were fanned from abroad, especially by Egypt and Syria, and Nasser called openly for the overthrow of the Lebanese government. The degree to which arms and guerrillas were being infiltrated into Lebanon was never adequately established, but that the government had reason to feel mortally threatened there can be no doubt. President Chamoun's request for intervention was at first ignored; then, when a coup toppled the friendly government of Iraq (a Communist-dominated military dictatorship resulted), American soldiers and Marines went across the beaches. Turkey, Iran and Pakistan (members of CENTO) applauded the decision.

Altogether, nearly 15,000 men went into Lebanon, with 25,000 more on seventy ships standing offshore. Not a shot was fired, and in three months the entire force had been withdrawn. With American help the warring factions had negotiated a peace which has so far survived, though it is now dangerously threatened by the Palestine guerrillas. The intervention was not popular either at home or abroad, but apart from saving the constitutionally elected government of Lebanon, the landing served a useful purpose. It demonstrated that the United States was still seriously interested in the Middle East at a time when, as a result of Suez, many people had come to believe that we were indifferent. Nine years of relative peace followed, Soviet penetration was slowed, Nasser's ambitions were curbed or diverted into other channels such as Yemen, and in all probability King Hussein's Jordan was granted a new lease on life. This is a lot to claim for one brief show of force, and of course none of it can be proven beyond doubt, but it seems more persuasive than the contention that the Lebanon landing, like all our interventions, accomplished nothing.

THE CONGO.   Of all the colonies which have achieved independence in the postwar period, the Democratic Republic of the Congo was the least prepared for it. Except for fairly widespread primary education, the Belgians had done virtually nothing to prepare the Congolese for the responsibilities they would assume. At the time of independence, June 30, 1960, there was not a single Congolese doctor, lawyer or engineer. Transportation, communications, every essential service, depended upon the Belgians; they also provided officers for the Force Publique, which, in a country with no sense of nationhood and three hundred tribes having ancient animosities, bore an awesome burden of maintaining public order. Within a week, the Force Publique had mutinied and the Congo was in a state of chaos.

Wisely, the United States declined an invitation from Premier Patrice Lumumba to intervene, realizing that this would bring the Cold War into the heart of Africa. Instead it threw its weight behind a U. N. operation of enormous size and complexity which for the next four years struggled with uneven success to hold the Congo together. We were the only one of the major powers that consistently (a) supported the central government which alone had even a claim to legitimacy, and (b) bent every effort to preserve the territorial integrity of the Congo, realizing that if this large (fourteen million) and potentially wealthy country in the very heart of Africa were to be fragmented by tribal animosities and European complicity, the consequences for the continent would be incalculable. The sorts of centrifugal pressures later seen in Nigeria would have been irresistible. With France opposing the U. N. operation, with the Soviet Union seeking by every means to obstruct it, with the Belgians, supported by the British, stubbornly thwarting its efforts to stop Moïse Tshombe's attempts to detach the incomparably rich Katanga province from the Congo, it is no small achievement to have preserved the integrity of the Congo. Yet three American Presidents persevered in this undertaking in the face of hostility and obstruction from both left and right, at home and abroad. Without the indispensable support of the United States, including more than half the U. N.'s costs of some $10 million a month, the operation would have ended in certain failure.

Despite Lumumba's increasingly outrageous behavior,* the United States supported his government, pressing hard for the departure of the Belgians, which was the Premier's first concern, and providing technical and financial assistance through the U. N., as well as most of the transport for the U. N. forces. Meanwhile, the Soviet Union was sending large numbers of technicians, aircraft and other arms, not through the U. N., but directly to Lumumba. Shortly after President Joseph Kasavubu dismissed Lumumba, the Russians and the Czechs were ordered out of the country, a measure that was to be repeated four years later.

---

* With his country in a state of anarchy, Lumumba told a press conference, "I will tell you what is at the bottom of the Congo crisis. The nations are jealous of our power and greatness." The United Nations, which was literally saving his skin (though it later failed), was the object of constant abuse, and when three Canadians were viciously beaten by Congolese soldiers, he first declined to apologize, then called the incident "banal" (*The New York Times,* August 21, 1960). The notion that the United States and/or the United Nations is accountable for Lumumba's murder is without foundation; in secrecy he was turned over by one set of enemies to a worse set of enemies for almost certain execution by Tshombe in Katanga, where the U. N.'s writ did not then run.

There then emerged in the Congo roughly three centers of power: the central government in Léopoldville, with Joseph Iléo and later Cyrille Adoula as premier; Katanga, where Tshombe, with the support of Belgian and British mining interests, was all-powerful; and the area around Stanleyville, where the political heirs of Lumumba, Albert Kalonji and Antoine Gizenga, proclaimed a "legal" government which had the support of the Communist bloc and the radical African states. The central government, supported by the Army under Colonel Joseph Mobutu, was prepared to negotiate a confederal constitution which would have given the provinces a high degree of autonomy. This was a compromise which Lumumba had refused to offer, but it proved insufficient to attract Tshombe. There followed years of effort to bring the warring parties together, and on several occasions a peaceful solution seemed to have been found. But each time what was thought to be agreement was broken by Tshombe, and it was not until January 1963 that the Katanga rebellion was put down by the U. N. by force of arms. Later that year, Premier Adoula formed a government of reconciliation which included Gizenga; but, wanting the whole cake or nothing, Gizenga never participated and remained in Stanleyville.

At their height, U. N. forces in the Congo numbered twenty thousand; on June 30, 1964, the last of them departed, and it was only through immense exertions by the American government and particularly our ambassador in Léopoldville that they were persuaded to remain so long. Yet even before their departure the situation was again deteriorating. In the preceding year a group of Congolese exiles had set up a Committee for National Liberation, without a program but with a determination to overthrow the Adoula government. Operating out of the Congo (Brazzaville) and Burundi, and supported by the Chinese Communists, they exploited growing terrorism in the eastern provinces and Katanga.

Three hours after the departure of the last U. N. soldier, President Kasavubu announced the resignation of Premier

Adoula to clear the way for parliamentary elections and a referendum on a new constitution. To the dismay of the United States and the disgust of many African states, the man appointed to head the transitional government was Tshombe. Much has been made of our subsequent support of his government, yet it was entirely consistent with our policy to do so, for he represented the only authority with any hope of holding the Congo together, and in his new role he represented the nearest thing to legitimacy available. Moreover, despite some very unattractive traits and policies, he was the most efficient leader in the Congo (which is not saying much) and, contrary to popular mythology, one of the very few who had substantial support outside his own tribe. When he returned to Léopoldville after the meeting of unaligned states in Cairo, at which Nasser had had the gall to imprison him, he was cheered by more than a quarter of a million Congolese in a city nearly a thousand miles from his own political base.

Nevertheless, the appointment of Tshombe intensified the Cold War by inflaming passions for and against him. The Soviet Union, Communist China, Ghana, Uganda, Algeria, Egypt, the Sudan, the Congo (Brazzaville) and Burundi began arming his enemies. Stanleyville fell to the rebels, and the Congolese Army seemed to be falling apart. Now, with the United Nations departed, the United States for the first time became deeply involved unilaterally. Over the summer of 1964 it sent trucks, communications equipment and four C-130 transport planes together with about a hundred Army and Air Force personnel to service them and guard them on the ground. In addition, it sent sixty-eight officers and men as advisers to the Congolese Army and followed this with several long-range reconnaissance planes and B-26 light bombers, but without pilots to fly them. Meanwhile, Tshombe was recruiting white mercenaries who were succeeding in putting together a small but efficient fighting force. By September it had recaptured Albertville and was moving on Stanleyville.

When Stanleyville was about to fall, the rebel leader and

head of the newly founded Congolese People's Republic government, Christophe Gbenye, announced that unless the advance was halted, the white population of eight hundred would be massacred. When last-minute negotiations failed and hope faded that the hostages would be spared, United States Air Force planes dropped four hundred Belgian paratroopers on the Stanleyville airport. In this and a similar operation at Paulis two days later by the Belgians alone, some two thousand foreigners—including four hundred Asians—were rescued, but approximately seventy were slaughtered as the Belgians entered the cities.

What appeared to the West as a humanitarian rescue operation was seen by the Africans generally as a vicious, racist act of colonialism, though it did not affect the outcome of the battle for Stanleyville, which was already surrounded. All that the United States had done in an earlier period to defeat Tshombe and to preserve the wealth of Katanga for all the Congo was forgotten as African delegates at the United Nations indulged themselves in what an aroused Adlai Stevenson described as "irrational, irresponsible, insulting and repugnant language."

In appraising this incident, it must be remembered that, with exceptions, the Belgians and other whites who had remained in or returned to the Congo were not colonialist exploiters of the wealth of the Congo. They were primarily low- and medium-grade technicians who were, and still are, essential to the Congo's functioning as a semideveloped society. If fear were to drive them out of the country, every hope of the Congo's fulfilling its potential would go with them. This is not, as it may seem to be, a reflection on the Congolese or even necessarily on the Belgians, though they were criminally negligent as colonial administrators. The fact is that in every African country—even the more advanced, like Ghana—the white population increased after independence, as a result of the powerful demand for technicians of all kinds.

With the recapture of Stanleyville, the civil war was by no means over and rebels still held a fifth of the country; but the situation had passed its nadir. Over the next eighteen months, outside intervention in the Congo markedly declined. Several of the African countries involved became resentful of Soviet and Communist Chinese influence. The Sudan soon decided it had nothing to gain by being a supply route to the rebels. The leftist government in Burundi was overthrown and the Chinese were ejected. With the removal of Ahmed Ben Bella in Algeria and Nkrumah in Ghana, the rebels lost two of their principal backers, while Nasser became increasingly involved in Yemen. Finally the situation was eased by the removal of Tshombe in late 1965 and the assumption of power by Mobutu as President and head of the government.

There was one further brief involvement of the United States in the Congo, and it is of considerable importance. In 1967 rebellion again broke out in Katanga, and again white mercenaries were hired, this time to fight against the central government. The United States sent three transport planes to assist Mobutu in moving his forces into position to quell the uprising. As with the earlier U. S. involvement, many members of the Senate were outraged. Senator Fulbright was "shocked, surprised and dismayed." Senator Richard B. Russell called the action "immoral" and "an unjustified intervention in a local disturbance." Perhaps so, but Africans did not think so. That the United States would help blacks to fight whites lifted it to a peak of popularity. Despite the fact that we had stood up to the Belgians and the British earlier in defense of the real interests of an independent Congo, it was not until this event that the Africans credited us with the capacity for impartiality. What is more important, when the planes were withdrawn five months later after the rebellion had been put down, it was generally agreed that the American assistance had again been critical in preserving the territorial integrity of the Congo, and that this simple gesture may have spared the lives of the seventy thousand law-abiding white residents of the Congo who would have been the victims of the race war that had been threatening.

The moral of this too-compressed story of the Congo struggle would seem to be that American intervention *can* be discriminating, limited and successful in terms of its objectives and of the interests of the indigenous people. It is a story of political courage and constancy by the American government. We worked through and with the United Nations for as long as it could be persuaded to maintain a presence; then we acted unilaterally, making a limited commitment, to offset the intervention of others. We did not "save" the Congo, but we gave it a chance to preserve its unity and thereby deterred the balkanization of other African states. Equally important, we protected the U. N. from disintegration by supporting—alone among the major powers—the U. N.'s only acceptable authority, the Secretary General.

Detractors have said that our only motive was to keep Communism out of the heart of Africa. This was certainly a factor and it may have been instrumental in keeping a balky Congress from bolting. But it does not explain the determination with which we opposed Tshombe, the darling of the militant anti-Communists, when he was trying to detach Katanga, and with it the wealth of the Congo. When Africans of later generations write their own history of this period, they will, I think, conclude that the United States well served the interests of the Congo and of all Africa. Whether American historians will conclude that the United States served its own interests equally well seems more problematical. It will be pointed out that our financial interests were negligible and our security interests minimal, and that we antagonized almost everyone. But Africa and the United Nations would be a lot worse off today if we had not played our part as we did.

In any event, the Congo illustrates the eternal dilemma of a superpower: Do you put your feet to the fire or do you try to put it out?

VIETNAM. Nothing that can be written about our most costly and disastrous intervention is likely to make the slightest dent in any individual's thinking. We have all made up our minds. Nor can one hope to add in a few words to what has been said in the millions that have been written. Nevertheless, if only for the sake of consistency and comparison with other American interventions, the subject cannot be avoided, but will be treated with the greatest brevity.

Vietnam is a tragedy of classic proportions in the literal Greek sense of the word. Out of good intentions crimes have been committed. A people who no longer believe in fate, who are persuaded they are masters of their own destiny, were led step by step into an abyss where means were no longer related to ends.

U. S. government officials and their critics have been equally guilty of self-deception. The former persuaded themselves that our vital interests were at stake (which they had not been); the latter convinced themselves that nothing was at stake (which there is). The government emphasized aggression by the North Vietnamese, while the critics stressed the civil-war aspect (which made them both right and both wrong). Officials overestimated progress; critics exaggerated the lack of it. The officials emphasized the enemy's rigidity; the critics claimed that, if the United States did such and such, the North Vietnamese response would be so-and-so—and in every case were proved wrong. The officials minimized the transgressions of the South Vietnamese government, and the critics idealized a North Vietnamese regime which had established itself by brutal force. Officials persuaded themselves that President Thieu is a great man and excused the inexcusable; the critics excoriated him, demanding virtues found in few if any Asian leaders, especially when their country was mortally threatened. Officials emphasized that Asian governments are strongly opposed to a precipitous withdrawal and favor a continuing U. S. presence in Asia; the critics stressed worldwide condemnation of the war. And so it goes.

Some thoughts and queries:

1. Vietnam is not the ugliest, the most reprehensible or even the most unpopular war we have fought, though it comes close on all three scores. By all accounts the War of 1812 and the Mexican War were more unpopular, and the latter was probably more reprehensible, since it was clearly for our own immediate gain, which Vietnam is not. The war in the Philippines was uglier, more savage. What especially distinguishes Vietnam is that it is the longest war in our history and it is the first war that the whole world has been witness to. If all societies were open societies, the television camera might become the ultimate weapon for keeping the peace. But since all societies are not open, what then?

2. What is meant by "No more Vietnams"? That we will never again assist a nation under attack? That next time we'll use nuclear weapons? That we'll send airmen but not soldiers? That we'll fight close to home but not far away? That we'll defend strong societies but not weak ones? That we'll help countries where we understand the culture, but not where we don't? That we'll fight declared but not undeclared wars? These are not academic questions.

3. If the North Vietnamese are just "good nationalists," what were they doing with 100,000 troops in Laos and Cambodia before U. S. entry there? It is no answer to say they were driven by the Americans to use these countries as sanctuaries. This may be true, but it does not explain why Communist Vietnamese have been fighting in Laos off and on since 1953, four years after Laotian independence, or why, more recently, scores of thousands of North Vietnamese have fought pitched battles with the legitimate government of Laos. In 1962 we accepted the neutralization of Laos reluctantly, doubting that it would be respected but hoping that it might establish a pattern which could be followed in the rest of Indochina. The provisions of the agreement were never observed by either the Laotian Communists, the Pathet Lao, or their North Vietnamese allies. Their mounting defiance of Laotian neutrality

ultimately led to our involvement, but only under the most intense provocation.

In Cambodia, Prince Sihanouk proved too clever by half.
So busy was he ingratiating himself with the Chinese and the
North Vietnamese that he compromised his neutrality and
drove his countrymen to revolt. Thus we had the double irony
of a royal prince, fun-loving and high-living, being lionized in
the capital of modern puritanism, Peking, the focus of his
fears, while the United States, which he did not fear and which
had respected his neutrality, invaded his country. Admittedly,
the war in Vietnam made the position of Cambodia exceed-
ingly difficult, and one would not be disposed to criticize
Sihanouk if he had not been adopted as a favorite of those
Americans who delight in believing every accusation of a foreign politician against the United States and who overlook the
fact that Sihanouk was more arbitrary than Thieu.

4. The hatred which many in this country display for Thieu
and Ky is very nearly as obsessive as that of the most impassioned anti-Communist toward Mao or Ho or Stalin. We can
abhor Thieu's political arrests without forgetting that even the
best of governments have thrown their enemies into prison in
time of war. We can be angered by Thieu's unwillingness to
broaden the base of his government, while realizing that most
political factions in South Vietnam want to avoid commitment
and would very probably refuse to join the present government,
not necessarily because they are so opposed to it, but because
they want to keep all their options open. We can regret that the
legislature is not more active or powerful, while noting that the
Senate has publicly stood up to Thieu and opposed him—an
inconvenience which was never suffered by Mao or Ho or Stalin.
We can condemn Thieu's failure to adopt reforms designed to
win popular support, while admitting that the land-reform program is one of the most liberal in the world. We can assert that
the Saigon government would not survive without American
support, while recognizing that it is an unprovable hypothesis
only and that other South Vietnamese governments have fallen

in spite of us. We can allege that Ky and Thieu are obstructing a political settlement, while acknowledging that they have made far more concessions than the North Vietnamese. We can even wish to see the collapse of the Thieu government, while allowing that Thieu may be as sincere in his convictions as was the late Ho Chi Minh in his.

5. In the last analysis, all commentary on Vietnam is now irrelevant unless it focuses on how to get out or how we got in. We must accomplish the former without delay, and for our own future security and social health we must comprehend the latter. Since each of these questions is too large to essay here, attention has been given to one corollary: that he who sees Vietnam in terms of stark blacks and whites does a great dis-service to his country and to understanding. If, after weighing all the evidence, one is persuaded that we ought to get out of Indochina with all possible dispatch, well and good. But if one argues that we ought to get out because we are inherently criminal while the North Vietnamese are virtuous and the South Vietnamese are undeserving of self-determination, then one's arguments are no more compelling than the arguments of those who are still carrying on anti-Communist crusades under the banner of righteousness.

It would be comforting to say, Never again—never will we send another American boy abroad to die. After Vietnam it is very easy to believe this. We have come full circle: war ac-complishes nothing, preserves nothing; it is destructive of everything, including our principles; it does not enhance our security, but merely tears the domestic fabric of our society.

There is much force in these arguments, though not all our military interventions would bear them out. A foreign observer and lifetime student of international-security affairs has offered at least a partial answer:

> International security is entering a dangerous phase. Hav-ing come to understand some of the problems of living with nuclear weapons, an older and more insidious threat is start-

ing to emerge. The powers which have been guaranteeing the security of small nations throughout the world are becoming perplexed and weary. They are beginning to question the purpose of it all. . . . In a few years, the aligned and neutralists, the large and the small, could find themselves living in a world in which security will depend on the size and efficiency of each country's own battalions. All the hopes of economic development could be lost if the great majority of weak nations could not rely on a security structure maintained with patient determination by the strong. . . . No one can predict what effect [the Vietnam] experience will have on America's view of the world: but there is a real danger that the wrong conclusions will be drawn and the United States will drastically reduce its support for the world security system. The consequences of this are appalling and could embark the world on a period of chaos and disorder such as it has not known for centuries.*

If, then, we cannot renounce the use of force in any and all circumstances, are there lessons that we can learn from our experience with intervention? Certainly we are unlikely to intervene *in force* again unless a vital national interest is quite obviously at stake. What has motivated a majority to remain silent would not apply in another such engagement. We can prevent gradual involvement beyond our original intentions by defining precisely the objective and interest involved and then sticking to them. We should keep the commitment limited and avoid involving the nation's prestige beyond what is absolutely necessary (and also avoid overvaluing prestige). We should not intervene precipitously: events may move fast but rarely as conclusively as they may appear to. Wherever possible the Administration should take time to consult Congress, to obtain regional approval and to achieve international support if not multilateral participation. If the circumstances change or the conditions under which we undertook a commitment are not fulfilled by those asking for our help, we must have the de-

* Leonard Beaton in *The Round Table*, July 1966, pp. 215-16.

termination to reassess the objective. In any event, our planning for getting out should receive as much attention as our plans for getting in. And we should make sure that the force is adequate for the job.

Advice is easy to give, hard to put into practice. As one high official said after his retirement, "I have moved from the rigorous world of decision to the luxurious world of opinion." One of those who made such a move not long ago was Robert McNamara, former Secretary of Defense, who noted some time before his departure (in his Montreal speech of May 1966) that since 1958 there had been 164 outbreaks of significant violence in the world and that the United States had been involved in seven. "If the United States has been the world's policeman," Paul Seabury has observed, "it has been cautiously shirking most of its beat."*

Finally, we should bend every effort to renew U. N. peace-keeping. That an international force under the aegis of the U. N. and composed of small and middle powers is preferable to unilateral action by the United States hardly needs to be labored. Others should be as convinced of this as we should. Yet dissatisfaction with the Congo operation, Nasser's demand that U. N. peace-keeping forces be removed from Egyptian soil in 1967 and the unwillingness of many nations, large and small, to pay the costs have combined to put the whole concept of international peace-keeping in disfavor. However, it may be time for another effort: there is now a somewhat greater confluence of Soviet and American interests; one of the chief obstacles, de Gaulle, is gone; most nations of the world are both dissatisfied with the United States as peace-keeper and worried at the prospect of American withdrawal from old commitments. For us to take the initiative would probably not be effective, but we could encourage others, making clear that we stood ready to bear a more than proportionate share of the

---

* "The Revolt Against Obligation," in *U. S. Foreign Policy: Perspectives and Proposals for the 1970's,* edited by Paul Seabury and Aaron Wildavsky (New York: McGraw-Hill, 1969), p. 5.

costs if necessary and to provide most of the transport, as in fact we have done in the past.

It is both harder and easier to deal with the question of our involvements, or nonmilitary interventions—harder because they are so extensive, easier because it is simply inconceivable that in this interconnected world the largest factor in it can simply drop out. We might call home our troops, close all our foreign bases, drop the Peace Corps, and we would still be the most involved of nations. In fact we cannot and will not do these things, for they were tried and found wanting in what we then conceived to be a far less dangerous world.

Therefore there is no useful purpose to be served in debating *whether* we should be involved, but what sorts of involvement are unwarranted and unavoidable. Some assert that our extensive commitments made sense immediately after World War II when Europe was gravely weakened, but that they are not justified today. Yet as Europe has regained strength and prosperity, the nations of Europe have steadily reduced their commitments abroad. France still maintains a presence in Africa but has withdrawn totally from Southeast Asia. As recently as 1962 Britain was expanding its base in Aden as though it intended to remain forever, but four years later it was gone. It has pulled out of Africa, and though the new Conservative government proposes to remain in the Persian Gulf and Singapore, its presence will be token at best. In these places Britain has exerted a steadying influence, preventing confrontations between small nations, restraining ancient animosities. Withdrawal has not been welcomed as an act of statesmanship, but has generally been regretted by those affected. The Soviet fleet is already replacing the British in the Indian Ocean, to the considerable alarm of Australians and others. Are the Soviets, by simple default, to be allowed to move in everywhere the European powers have withdrawn their restraining presence? Almost without exception the non-Communist countries of Asia have urged the United States not to reduce its commitments there in any significant degree.

This is only one reason why our options are more limited than they may first appear. In any event, the topic is too large to discuss here except in terms of a few principles which will illustrate some of the dilemmas.

The first is that involvement is a two-sided coin where disengagement or inaction is involvement on another plane. South Africa offers an example. In international affairs, it is a hostile act to cut off trade and investment. To do so without overt provocation (as we felt in the case of Cuba) is certainly to become involved in the domestic affairs of another nation. Of course, we are profoundly involved in trade and investment with countries whose governments we deplore, and we do not consider halting such contacts. Should we have done so in the case of South Africa? Is it excusable for Americans to make fat profits from a system of human injustice which the United States officially condemns? Human injustice and exploitation are no strangers to this earth; what makes South Africa distinctive is that it is the only country (now joined by Rhodesia, which we do not recognize) where racialism is official policy— instigated, promoted and enforced by the government. To cut off investment and trade with South Africa today would be merely a gesture having no influence on South Africa, though it would have the merit of squaring our actions with our principles and protestations.* But in 1960 after the Sharpeville massacre, in which sixty-nine black Africans were killed by police and about 180 wounded, the effect might have been different. White South Africans were badly shaken, their police state was far less efficient then and they were economically less self-sufficient. Restriction on trade and investment at that time— even a statement by the President that the American government considered trade and investment ill-advised—*might* have

* In May 1970, the United States announced that it would actively discourage trade and investment in South West Africa, the U. N. trust territory administered by South Africa and incorporated into its system of apartheid. Among other things, the U. S. government will not assist American investors "against claims of a future lawful Government of Namibia [the African name for the territory]."

had some effect in marginally changing the direction of the South African government. But it would have represented the kind of intervention which most governments are loath to undertake (and not merely for financial reasons) and which most of our present critics of government would oppose in other instances.

Another principle is that, once we are involved, powerful arguments can be marshaled for further involvement. Observe the Philippines, a country for which we feel—or have felt—a special responsibility as the former colonial power, and where total disengagement would mean disaster for the Filipinos. One of the principal ways in which we express this special relationship is to grant the Philippines the largest sugar quota of any country in the world—larger than they can fill—at prices that are substantially above the world average. The beneficiaries of this largesse are a relative handful of big landowners who may well be the most intolerable exploiters in the world today. The cane cutters, the largest group of agricultural workers in an overwhelmingly agricultural country, do not have enough to eat, live in the most appalling conditions and must put their children to work at the age of fourteen or fifteen in order to survive. Ostensibly there is a minimum wage of one dollar a day, but it is rarely observed and never enforced, and the average is sixty cents a day or less. The foreign exchange which the Philippines derives from the sale of sugar to the United States is essential to its survival, but the lush profits of the planters are not. Are we justified in being, indirectly, a party to this human exploitation? Should we not insist that we will not buy sugar cut by laborers who do not receive a living wage? If we do, we will unquestionably be interfering in the domestic affairs of another nation; indeed, corruption being what it is in the Philippines, we might have to have our own inspectors with right of access to the cane fields. But since we set other requirements for the things we import—such as the purity of refined sugar—don't we have an obligation, as the sole purchaser of Philippine sugar, to see that human degradation is not part of the price we pay for it? Extreme poverty is not always avoidable; in this instance it is inexcusable.* In a country that may explode at any time, can we afford to become more deeply involved? Can we afford not to?

A third principle is that involvements, once undertaken, are difficult to withdraw from, though changed circumstances may have made them inadvisable or obsolete. Whether the CENTO and SEATO pacts† should ever have been undertaken is debatable, but they seem to have very little utility now, and many consider them defunct. Neither provides for binding defense commitments, as NATO does, and both conduct worthwhile ventures little related to defense. Yet if the United States were to withdraw, a number of countries would feel a profound unease. Therefore our inclination is to let matters drift along on mounting irrelevance and ambiguity.

Similarly, our arrangement with Portugal for the use of the Azores made some sense in the era of short-range, propeller-driven planes, but seems a bad bargain today, for it appears to restrict the pressure we can bring to bear on Portugal to alter her policies in Africa. There are a fair number of obsolete arrangements of this kind where we pay a high political price for a small return. They are hard to change, for each has its constituency within the American bureaucracy and abroad, and it is always easier to do nothing than to do something. But our obligations and commitments do need to be reexamined, not in the spirit of seeing where we can escape tiresome burdens, but in an effort to see that they remain consistent with the world as it is today and with our real interests.

* To acknowledge that we too exploit our agricultural labor does not weaken the case; both problems deserve attention. Moreover, the instruments available here—strikes, enforced minimum-wage laws, public opinion that can carry political weight, etc.—are simply not available in the Philippines.

† CENTO consists of the United Kingdom, Turkey, Iran and Pakistan (Iraq having withdrawn in 1959); the United States is not a member but participates in its committees. SEATO consists of Australia, France, New Zealand, Pakistan, the Philippines, Thailand, the United Kingdom and the United States.

VI

What Is the National Interest?

PEOPLE OFTEN speak of the national interest as though it were a sort of Rosetta Stone, providing answers to all the most perplexing questions of foreign policy. For some critics it is enough to assert that a particular policy is not in our national interest to establish that the policy is bad.

But deciding upon the national interest is what politics is all about. And deciding how to promote that interest is what policy-making is all about. Professor Kenneth Boulding has rightly pointed out that "the national interest is a variable and not a constant. The national interest is what the nation is interested in."*

Vital interests often conflict with other interests which some may feel are no less urgent: for example, national defense is a vital interest which conflicts with the urgent need to preserve a larger share of our resources for domestic use. We have an interest in seeing an end to apartheid in South Africa, but it is not so vital as to demand the use of force. Originally, we went into Vietnam in defense of the principle of free choice—that those who manifestly wanted to defend themselves against Communist aggression and subversion would have our help. It

* *American Militarism 1970*, edited by Erwin Knoll and Judith Nies McFadden (New York: Viking, 1969), p. 90.

107

was only later, when it was apparent that Saigon would collapse without our physical intervention, that we asserted that
our own national security—that is to say, a vital interest—was
involved. Whether those who pronounced this really believed
it at the time or whether they thought it necessary to justify so
heavy an expenditure of men and materiel is not altogether
clear; but it came to be believed by many. It wholly altered the
terms and conditions of our involvement and the difficulty of
withdrawal.

The moral is that references to the national interest should
be treated with the greatest skepticism, for the term can become
a refuge both for those who wish to defeat sound policies and
for those who want to excuse bad ones. If it were self-evident
what the national interest was and how it could be attained,
Congress could complete its annual business in a few months
and the Washington bureaucracy could be cut in half.

It would be well if we could ban the term "national interest"
except as it is used to distinguish the interests of the whole
from the selfish or parochial interests of groups within the
society. When American businessmen abroad assert that what
is good for them is good for the United States, it can fairly be
pointed out that high profits, low rates of reinvestment, support of conservative governments and the like are not necessarily in the national interest. This is not to say that those who
try to identify personal or group interest with the national interest always act from purely selfish motives. Misguided as was
the Committee of One Million, which for years lobbied successfully against rational policies toward Communist China,
many of its most effective members were moved by a genuine
love of the Chinese people and a belief that we bore a share of
the responsibility for a terrible fate that had befallen them. A
more recent example is the effort of a segment of the American
Roman Catholic hierarchy to induce the United States to intervene on the side of predominantly Catholic Biafra against
predominantly Muslim Nigeria. Perhaps the most obvious case

is that of Americans—not all of them Zionists—who urge a more active American role in the defense of Israeli interests. In short, one's concept of the national interest is an amalgam of personal and group interests, prejudices, values, priorities, fears and view of the nation itself. Obvious as this seems, it is often forgotten.

One should not lament this plethora of interest groups or their efforts to influence policy. Since the most intelligent and informed of men without axes to grind—even those of the same generation and basic experience—differ fundamentally in their conception of the national interest, there is no security in placing our faith in some Platonic version of philosopher kings. Henry Wriston has made the point that the real "invisible government" in the United States is not the sinister thing the term suggests, but consists of the infinite number of voluntary organizations and *ad hoc* groups which seek to exercise political influence and in the process serve an invaluable educative function.* And where neither of the major political parties has a coherent outlook and its members are free of the discipline characteristic of parliamentary systems, these voluntary groups become almost essential to getting things done. Out of all their shifting pressures, and counterpressures may emerge the best hope of a consensus which will be in the national interest.

Supposing that we can regain a consensus as to what sort of world we want to live in, the more difficult problem is then to determine what responsibility we have, if any, for trying to achieve it. In international affairs it is assumed that each nation behaves in its self-interest, but some define that interest in terms of intense nationalism or narrow advantage, while other countries see their self-interest being served by broad cooperation among states and find their own advantage in the strengthening and development of other countries.

* Wriston, *Diplomacy in a Democracy* (New York: Harper, 1956), pp. 108-9.

Differences in conception of the national interest, then, often stem from differing answers to the question, To what extent are our interests tied to the interests of others? And to what extent are the interests of others tied to ours? The network of commitments which we undertook after the war were based on the premise that there was a high degree of mutuality of interest among a majority of nations, and it was because this view was widely reciprocated that we became heavily involved. No one who has read Dean Acheson's *Present at the Creation* can imagine him testing every issue by a conventional standard of the national interest which pitted American interests against those of Britain and France. He saw them as interlocked in so fundamental a way as to make it possible to overcome differences of outlook, of experience and even of immediate interests. Because of discrepancies in wealth and power, we perhaps did more than we ought, and others less. And some came to doubt the original premise—notably France under de Gaulle.

To be sure, the world has changed, and the confluence of interest is neither so real nor so apparent as it was in the fifties. But neither have the purposes for which immediate interests were often submerged in a larger concern lost their validity.

The United States, no less than its allies, has on occasion overridden or ignored the interests of individual partners—sometimes in the genuine belief that it was acting in the interests of the majority, sometimes out of narrower motives of self-interest. Ironically, many of our domestic critics are now making the same error of assuming to speak for others in asserting that the mutuality of interest was or is without foundation or that other nations want to end the relationship. Some may, others clearly don't, and in reassessing our commitments one of the problems will be to decide how to weigh the desires and anxieties of other nations.

What has characterized Americans' definition of the national interest in the postwar period is the assumption that interests impose obligations—that since our interests are so intimately tied with those of others, we have obligations not different in kind but different in degree from those of others by virtue of our wealth, power and geographic advantage. Even making allowance for the rhetoric of which American leaders are overly fond, this assumption is reflected in the statements of every President and every Secretary of State in the past thirty years. This, presumably, is what today's radical critics particularly quarrel with; they interpret this assumption, or the words in which it finds expression, as self-righteous and hypocritical. But this is an injustice to the American people, if not to their leaders. Much of the idealism and moral fervor which the younger generation today directs toward the solution of domestic problems was in an earlier generation directed outward upon a world which seemed desperately in need of help. It is difficult for many of today's adults to comprehend how their motives can be so disparaged. No doubt there was some self-delusion, but is this not part of the human condition?

It is well to bear in mind that individuals may arrive at similar views of the national interest from totally different directions; or they may differ totally in their views of the national interest while holding a similar set of values. For example, all through the late forties and early fifties when our present battery of commitments was being formulated, there was a body of American opinion which was totally opposed. Led by such men as Senator Robert A. Taft and Senator John C. Stennis, they were not a group with whom today's radical critics could comfortably identify. They believed that the United States would spend itself into penury and that the economy would have to be so regulated as to be indistinguishable from socialism. They offered instead the concept of Fortress America: let America be strong, but let the rest of the world take care of itself. For them this was the national interest.

One of the shortcomings of the concept of national interest is that it implies an orderliness in the process of formulating policy and action which rarely exists. Like all collective endeavors, policy-making is a process of bargaining both within the executive branch and between the executive branch and Congress, with each of the innumerable participants reflecting segments of American opinion as well as his own predilections. What emerges may or may not be a distillation of the national interest from a purely rational point of view, but it will almost always be declared to be so.

Despite overwhelming evidence to the contrary, it is widely believed today that the United States acts from one of two motivations, and two only: national security and commercial advantage. One has only to glance at the Middle East to realize how much more complex our motives are.

By neither of these criteria can it be considered to have been in the national interest to support the creation of Israel or to give even the appearance of taking its side in subsequent conflicts with its Arab neighbors. We have financial interests in the Arab world running into billions of dollars, and perhaps no area of the world is so important to us in preserving our balance of payments. As a nation, we have no remotely equivalent economic interest in Israel.

Similarly, the Arab states stand astride two continents and occupy what has tritely but truly been called the crossroads of the world, an area of great strategic importance in terms of geography as well as oil. Israel is a mere dot on the world map and without significant natural resources. Yet we have stood by Israel, as we must, at least to the extent of insisting that the Arab states recognize its right to exist and of giving it part of the arms required to defend itself. This of course has antagonized the Arabs, driving them toward the Soviet Union. As a result the Russians have been given a foothold in the eastern Mediterranean, which it has been our established purpose to prevent.

Whether we should have supported the creation of Israel or whether its creation would have been possible if the world had not been caught up in a moment of collective guilt is now beside the point. The deed cannot be undone. Out of unselfish motives grave injustice was done the Palestinian Arabs, and a fierce, unyielding hostility created where none existed. It has been cynically fanned by the Russians, although they supported the creation of Israel and were among the first of the great powers to recognize the new state. Whether or not in the past we have been as even-handed as we ought in trying to quash the fires in the Middle East, our efforts in this direction are made increasingly difficult by the Soviets' overt partisanship and refusal to agree to arms limitations. Nor has the fact that we backed Nasser in the 1956 Suez crisis and have given very substantial aid to most of the Arab countries, including Egypt, appeared to affect the Arabs' judgment that we are against them.

Different people profess to find a variety of lessons in this trying and explosive situation. Some say it illustrates that there is no place for morality in the formulation of foreign policy, although oddly many who urge the most hard-nosed, restricted definition of the national interest are often precisely those who want us vigorously to support Israel. Conversely, many of those who talk most about the need for greater morality in American policy commit themselves to the Arab cause and would have us abandon Israel. Just how this would demonstrate a higher morality is difficult to comprehend. The irony, however, is clear: the moralists tend to urge support of the Arabs with whom our commercial and security interests lie, while the realists incline to urge support of Israel where we have only a moral obligation and a conviction that the first right of any nation is survival.*

* The supposition that U. S. policy in the Middle East is dictated by "the Jewish vote" no longer corresponds with reality, if it ever did. Although sympathy for Israel has declined somewhat since it ceased to appear as the un-

Meanwhile, those in government who bear the burdens and responsibilities of making decisions strive for a balanced resolution of irreconcilable interests, thereby satisfying no one— as must inevitably be the case. They know better than most that the tragedies and dilemmas they inherit, as well as the achievements, may have been born of decisions made almost without reference to the national interest as such, or by a definition of it so broad as to far transcend the conventional criteria of security and economic advantage. Rather, we are motivated in our foreign policies by a complicated mix of interests which refuse to be boiled down to a few essences.

It is ironic that leftist intellectuals should be among those who define the national interest most narrowly. Whether they are describing what they believe it is seen to be by "the power structure," or whether they are describing what it ought to be, the definition tends to be unimaginative, unexciting and heavily circumscribed. On the other hand, a representative of that scorned breed, the middle-aged Washington bureaucrat, has written:

> No one's national interest is self-defining. It is a kind of UFO—an unidentified flying object. It is a label for uninspired policies pursued by uninspired men. By definition, national interest, whatever it is, lacks primary interest to others. For America this is particularly self-defeating, because we thereby thoughtlessly discard our unique historic reputation for dis-

derdog, Americans favor Israel over the Arabs by a ratio of 15 to 1, according to a 1970 Gallup poll. President Nixon's hurried flight to New York to appease President Pompidou after pro-Israelis had demonstrated against him belies the contention that an American government will never offend the Jews. Moreover, the toughness with which we have treated Israel is remarkable. In an effort to impose some restraint on the Middle East arms race, we held up shipments to Israel for nearly two years while the Russians poured planes and missiles into Egypt and involved their own pilots and missile crews in combat situations. We yielded only when Egypt and the Soviet Union flagrantly broke a cease-fire agreement, thereby altering the strategic balance and making a mockery of our guarantee to Israel that the cease-fire would be observed.

interestedness. Hitherto that has been one of our most important national assets. . . . Lincoln, Wilson and Roosevelt at moments of supreme national crisis made our national interest interesting to others by identifying us with ideas that move mankind. And they were not just applying cosmetics to power. They were credible, because they thought the way they talked. Language was close to life, propaganda to performance, public relations to personal commitment.*

* Thomas L. Hughes, "On the Causes of Our Discontents," *Foreign Affairs,* July 1969, p. 666. Mr. Hughes, now President of the Foreign Policy Association, was formerly Director of Intelligence and Research in the State Department.

VII

"Economic Domination of the World"

ONE OF the central themes of the severer critics of American foreign policy is quite simply that the United States wishes to dominate the world and that it endeavors to achieve this goal primarily by the exercise of its economic power. Our every act, from foreign aid to the war in Vietnam, is explained by the exclusive dominance of business and financial interests in the formulation of policy. In our ruthless pursuit of needed raw materials and expanding markets it is the Third World in particular which we exploit and seek to subject to our control.

Two circumstances give the appearance of support to this thesis: first, the American economy is indeed overwhelmingly large and therefore has a heavy impact on other nations; and, second, having a private-enterprise economy, our traders and businessmen are interested in making profits. For some this seems sufficient evidence that we are also exploitative and practice economic imperialism on a massive scale. But do not all nations—socialist or capitalist, industrialized or underdeveloped—expect to derive some benefit from trade and investment, whether or not it is measured in purely economic terms? Implicit in the writing of the revisionists is the notion that the United States is alone in seeking to profit from international transactions. Surely there is nothing shameful in taking economic interests into account in formulating foreign policy. The question is whether our advantage is others' loss. This is the point that has not been established by critics in any broad or conclusive way. Why should it be presumed that the age-old concept of commerce as benefiting all parties to a transaction does not apply where the United States is involved? The revisionist critics have failed to show either in what manner we exploit other nations as a matter of policy or how American business exerts its domination over all other domestic interest groups in making foreign policy.

Later in this chapter we will examine some of the ways that American business abroad does fail to be sufficiently responsive to the interests of other nations and, indeed, to the U. S. national interest. Here it may be useful to pursue the arguments of the revisionists somewhat further. One of the elders of this predominantly young group is William Appleman Williams, an economic-determinist best known for his thesis that the United States has been solely responsible for the Cold War. In *The Tragedy of American Diplomacy,* published in 1957, he asserts that the most important policy of this century was (and is) that of the Open Door, seen not as an effort to compete on equal terms with European trading rivals, but as a means of imposing our imperial will on weak nations.

> It is vital to realize [Williams writes] that the Open Door Policy was derived from the proposition that America's overwhelming economic power [in the 1890s?] would cast the economy and politics of the weaker, underdeveloped countries in a pro-American mold. . . . The philosophy and practice of secular empire that was embodied in the Open Door Notes became the central feature of American foreign policy in the twentieth century.

Even the desire for peace had no other motive than American commercial advantage (earlier radicals, of course, held that businessmen sought war, not peace), especially "since American leaders feared war as the hothouse of revolution." We entered the First World War, he asserts, only because otherwise we would have had "to abandon [our] determination and destiny to lead the world." Williams even tries to show that those who opposed the League of Nations and those who favored it did so for the same reason—namely, "American imperial expansion."

In Williams' discourse, "trade" becomes a dirty word. He does not acknowledge that trade may be of mutual benefit, nor does he trouble to show how terms of trade were unfavorable (as they sometimes were and are); it is simply implied. He speaks of "Christian imperialism" as though foreign missions and Christian proselytizing were uniquely American phenomena.

It is fashionable today to deride Woodrow Wilson, but Williams goes so far as to paint him as intellectually dishonest and hypocritical, a fraud who was "seen through" in his own day by the peoples of the world.* Like all our Presidents from McKinley to Franklin D. Roosevelt and beyond, he was the creature of bankers and leaders of "the corporate structure," the only significant influence on policy. These corporate leaders are made to appear demoniacal in the single-mindedness with which they pursued measures of exclusive benefit to the United States. Where we had relations with the Soviet Union in the thirties, it was out of desire for "economic penetration"; where we did not, it was from animosity to revolution.†

* D. F. Fleming, who shares Williams' view that the United States is responsible for the Cold War, differs sharply with regard to Wilson. "The crushing of Wilson," he writes in *The Cold War and Its Origins* (New York: Doubleday, 1961, p. 1037), ". . . was in all probability the most decisive error in American history."

† In the light of Williams' denial of any U. S. right to play a significant role in the world, the following passage is especially significant: "By the end of Hoover's term in office, it was apparent that the broad revolutionary challenges to America's program for the world seemed to have survived and converged in a *Russia beginning to assert its right and ability to lead the world* out of the economic and spiritual depression into a better future." (Italics added.) By what measure the Soviet Union has such a "right," which when asserted by the United States is "imperialism" and "tragedy," the reader is left to surmise. And if the Soviets have a right to lead the world which we do not and which we have sought to deny them, then it follows quite logically that the United States has been responsible for the Cold War.

If the United States was in fact imperialistic and interventionist in the twenties and thirties, at a time when most of us thought it was isolationist, then it follows that we must be so today, when our power is far greater and our involvements have obviously increased. On the other hand, Gabriel Kolko, another revisionist who owes much to Williams, sees American imperialism as an essentially postwar phenomenon. He compares our relative self-sufficiency in the past with the present omnivorous demand of our industries for raw materials, especially minerals.* He points out that every ton of steel includes thirteen pounds of manganese, which must be imported, adding that half of the manganese of the world is in China and the Soviet Union and that China also has two thirds of the world's tungsten. If, as he asserts, access to these minerals dictates all our foreign policies, how is one to explain our policies toward these countries and our reluctance to trade with them?

No one doubts that the world is becoming increasingly interdependent, but to portray trade as the be-all and end-all of American foreign policy makes no sense. We are one of the few countries which could survive without trade; for many other nations, such as Britain and Japan, trade is a matter of life and death; its absence would mean strangulation and starvation. Two-way trade represents less than 5 percent of our gross national product—not an insignificant figure, but hardly a basis for spinning theories about the special dependence of the United States.†

In any event, it has not been that great imperial domain which Williams asserts the United States carved for itself in Asia and Latin America to which U. S. trade and investment have primarily flowed. Increasingly, it has been to Europe, Canada and the other developed countries. Frantz Fanon un-

* Kolko, *The Roots of American Foreign Policy* (Boston: Beacon, 1969), pp. 50-55.

† In 1970, in *The Roots of the Modern American Empire,* Williams reiterated the same thesis that (as paraphrased by a reviewer for *The New York Times*) "the single key to every action is the conscious desire to expand the marketplace for American goods."

derstood this. "It is a fact," he wrote, "that young nations do not attract much capital. . . . The spectacular flight of capital is one of the most constant phenomena of decolonization."* If Williams' thesis were correct, how could American businessmen for so long remain passive when the vast potential markets of China, the Soviet Union and Eastern Europe were arbitrarily closed to them by their own government? And is our attitude and behavior so unique that the experience of other "capitalist" countries is irrelevant? If, as Williams and others contend, it is control and domination we seek as well as access to markets, then their definition of imperialism must have something in common with colonialism. The European powers discovered to their surprise not only that they did not need their colonies to survive, but that they prospered immensely without them. In the last analysis, General de Gaulle was able to get out of Algeria because Frenchmen finally grasped that Algeria was a net financial loss—even without war. Japan discovered that domination of East Asia was not required for its prosperity, but that, confined within its home islands, it could achieve and sustain a growth rate of better than 10 percent a year until it had become the third industrial power in the world. Why should it be supposed that the U. S. economy requires warmaking, while the fastest-growing economy in the world has virtually no military establishment at all? Indeed, Japan's freedom from the burden of its own defense is believed to be one of the chief causes of its economic success.

That American investment abroad is enormous and often has an overwhelming impact on the economies and even the politics of other countries cannot be denied. The United States Council of the International Chamber of Commerce estimates that the total output resulting from these investments is in excess of $200 billion.† If this were looked upon as a separate

* Fanon, *The Wretched of the Earth* (New York: Grove Press, Evergreen paperback edition), p. 103.

† This figure is comparable to gross national product (GNP). Actual direct private investment abroad in 1969 was approximately $71 billion (book value).

"economy" it would be the third largest in the world. But more than two thirds of it is in the developed world,* and the share held by the developing countries has declined steadily throughout the postwar period. Between 1950 and 1968 the proportion of direct private investment in the less developed countries fell from 48 to 29 percent of the total, and the figure is undoubtedly lower today. During this period American investment in the advanced countries increased by a factor of eight, while in the developing countries it rose at half that rate. Even petroleum investments are larger in the developed countries, though 42 percent of all American private investment in the developing world is in oil.

With respect to trade, the picture is substantially the same. In the period 1967–69, American exports to the less developed world were more than twice the 1951–55 average, but as a percentage of our total exports they declined from 41 to 32 percent, in spite of foreign aid. As for imports from the developing world, they have grown relatively slowly. Whereas in the early fifties more than half our imports were from the less developed countries, by the late sixties their share had fallen to 28 percent and was declining steadily. Surprisingly, in 1969 manufactured imports from the less developed countries amounted to $2.8 billion (most of it, to be sure, from a relatively few countries), about the same as food and not far behind oil and metals combined.

These figures hardly sustain the Williams hypothesis—which has been adopted by Students for a Democratic Society and others as revealed truth—that the demands of the American economy require exploitation of weak and undeveloped countries, even control of them. Most nations of the Third World have nothing that is essential to us. Among those that do have critical minerals, one can trace no pattern of exclusive U. S.

---

* The developed countries are here defined as Western Europe including Finland, Greece, Portugal, Spain, Turkey and Yugoslavia, plus Canada, Japan, Australia, New Zealand and South Africa. I am indebted to Helena Stalson of the Council on Foreign Relations for the figures on which the calculations on this and subsequent pages are based.

domination. The notion that we are in Indochina to protect our economic interests is patently absurd. Those interests are virtually nil, and the wealth of Indochina is almost entirely in its soil. *Our investments in all of the Third World combined are less than we have been spending in Vietnam in eight months.* Our two-way trade (export plus imports) with the less developed world is less than we have been spending in Vietnam in nine months. If this is not sufficiently convincing, we have had the testimony of the president of the largest bank in the world that the war in Vietnam was bringing the American economy to ruin. In support of this thesis, the stock market has unfailingly risen with any hint of peace and fallen whenever the war was broadened or escalated.

There is good reason for this. Between 1961 and 1965, a period of comparative peace, corporate profits rose 61.2 percent; from the beginning of the Vietnam escalation to June 1970, corporate profits, adjusted for inflation, fell 16.8 percent. Similarly, the value of corporate stocks, which rose 48.5 percent in the 1961–65 period, fell by 36.5 percent between 1965 and June 1970.* In the face of such conclusive figures, how can one seriously contend that we are in Vietnam for economic reasons? To do so one must at the very least subscribe to the domino theory, so generally rejected today, and especially by the harshest critics of the war. To imagine that our Vietnam policies have been dictated by the need for Malaysian tin or Indonesian oil is to enter a world of fantasy.

The sad facts are that the developed countries offer more tempting markets and more favorable conditions for investment than do the less developed nations, and that by far the largest increases in both trade and investment have been in the field of manufacturing within the industrialized world. Whatever valuable or indispensable items we import from the Third World, they do not come from Indochina. It is just barely con-

---

* These figures are from a study of the war's costs by Professor Robert Eisner of Northwestern University.

ceivable that if we were to retreat into isolationism, the Soviet Union and its allies might corner the world market on some precious metal. But surely no one can seriously suppose that this remote contingency motivates American foreign policy or the outward thrust of American enterprise. It is true that the industrialized world cannot, without serious adjustment, get along without the oil of the less developed world, though others are more dependent on petroleum imports than we are (and we will be less so when the Alaskan fields begin producing). But though the oil-producing states have greatly increased their bargaining power with the international oil companies in recent years, it is not likely that they could avoid selling their principal product to Europe, Japan and the other big consumers, though the specter of the Soviet Union controlling all the oil of the Middle East disturbs many people. What makes the Third World particularly vulnerable economically is that a substitute can be found for almost every raw material, at a price—petroleum not excluded. The producers of cotton and rubber have long since learned to their anguish what synthetics can do to their markets. The greatest war in history was fought with the major combatants largely cut off from their normal sources of external supply. Thus the dependence of the industrialized nations on the Third World is much less than the reverse. On this score, as on so many others, the leaders of the less developed nations do not share the illusions of many Americans, or of Frantz Fanon, who did so much to shape them.

Fanon has created the impression that the Third World has powerful leverage against the Western world. If, he wrote,

the Third World is in fact abandoned and condemned to regression or at least to stagnation by the selfishness and wickedness of Western nations, the underdeveloped peoples will decide to continue their evolution inside a collective autarky. Thus the Western industries will quickly be deprived of their overseas markets. The machines will pile up their products in the warehouses and a merciless struggle will ensue on the European market between the trusts and the financial groups.

The closing of factories, the paying off of workers and unemployment will force the European working class to engage in an open struggle against the capitalist regime. Then the monopolies will realize that their true interests lie in giving aid to the underdeveloped countries—unstinted aid with not too many conditions.*

As we have seen, the developed nations simply are not dependent on the Third World to this degree, even if the less developed countries could achieve such remarkable cooperation as Fanon suggests. So we shall have to assist the less developed countries because it is the right thing to do and because it is in our long-term interest—not because of political and economic pressures that can be brought to bear against us.

But even Fanon recognized that, with a few exceptions, the nations of the Third World need more American (and other) investment, not less. The exceptions are the relatively few and fortunate countries with extraordinary mineral wealth, such as Chile or Saudi Arabia, where American involvement in the development of that resource has been too exclusive. But even these countries need more investment if it is diversified. In several important countries U. S. investment is minimal—for example, $300 million in India, a nation of 550 million people. Yet far from increasing appreciably, American investment in India is being withheld in such all-important fields as fertilizer. A few years ago, most of the major American oil and chemical companies were laying plans for large fertilizer-manufacturing operations in India. Only one has been brought to completion, and this has been a financial failure; all the others have been dropped after large expenditures. The principal reasons are the difficulties of dealing with the Indian bureaucracy, the inadequacy of the means of distribution and an inability to solve the problem of consumer credit, which is essential for the agricultural community in poor nations. The result may well be that the so-called green revolution promised by the new

* Fanon, *op cit.*, pp. 104-5.

seed discoveries of recent years will simply make the rich farmers richer (because they can pay cash for fertilizer) and the poor farmers poorer (because they will not be able to compete with the growers using the new seed).

And if foreign private investment is sluggish in India, where there is a huge potential market, what can be expected in the impoverished countries where the population is a few million or less? According to the World Bank, there are thirty-three sovereign nations in which the per-capita GNP is less than $100 a year. Unless they can produce for export, their prospects for development do not look bright. For perhaps a third of the nations of the world, "exploitation" is a remote but desired possibility. Meanwhile, through no one's fault or calculated selfishness, the prices they obtain for their coffee or peanuts or whatever remain relatively constant or possibly decline, while the prices they pay for almost everything they need for development may be counted upon to rise steadily. This is perhaps the central dilemma of underdevelopment.

It is on account of this phenomenon that the Third World has so earnestly wished to industrialize, and one of the commonest accusations against the United States and the former colonial powers is that we have discouraged industrialization to keep the new nations weak and to keep the prices of raw materials low. In the postwar period, at least, this impression has perhaps been caused by our reaction to two tendencies in the new nations: (1) to seek industrialization for its own sake, without considering whether it can be made efficient and therefore competitive; and (2) to neglect agriculture—both food and export crops. The United States has not discouraged industrialization in the Third World, but has pointed out that to manufacture for $4,500 a car which can be imported for $2,500 is not a sound route to development. Similarly, we have pointed out that to neglect established export products means a decline in all-important foreign exchange; and to neglect food crops at a time of burgeoning populations means that foreign exchange needed for other things will have to be

used to import food. The wisdom of this counsel has now begun
to sink in and the less developed countries are becoming much
more realistic in applying their resources in a balanced way.

Understandably, however, they point out that their infant
industries cannot initially compete with the established industries of the more advanced nations, and they demand that the
industrialized nations eliminate tariffs and quotas on their
manufactured products. After six years of discussion in
UNCTAD (United Nations Conference on Trade and Development), the industrialized nations agreed in October 1970 to
grant such preferences for a period of ten years. However, tariffs will not be reduced or removed on all manufactures—the
United States, for example, proposes to except textiles, shoes
and oil products—and much will depend on the liberality of national legislatures in giving the agreement real effect.

The high expectations which the less developed countries
have for the results of trade preferences have not been justified
by experience. Unrestricted access to the markets of the industrialized world, they assume, will markedly increase their exports of all kinds and encourage infant industries which at
present cannot compete. But where nations have in fact enjoyed such opportunities the expected benefits have not ac-
crued. In some instances "regional preferences . . . hindered
rather than helped development by obscuring the need for internal reforms and by orienting these countries toward high-
cost production for an artificially protected preferential market
rather than for competitive sales in world markets at large."*
Nevertheless, for reasons which are more political than economic, a system of worldwide preferences seems highly desirable if it can be achieved with a minimum of exceptions. The
United States was instrumental in reaching the present agreement, as it was in negotiating earlier tariff reductions in the so-

---

* W. Michael Blumenthal, "A World of Preferences," *Foreign Affairs,*
April 1970, p. 551. Despite this passage, Mr. Blumenthal, the U. S. negotiator
in the Kennedy Round, favors preferences provided they are on a worldwide
basis.

called Kennedy Round. The American market has been the most open in the world. Now the tide of protectionism is rising once again, starting with textiles and spreading dangerously into other sectors. It will be tragic and quite possibly disastrous if more than three decades of liberalizing trade legislation is wiped out. It can only retard global economic development and the processes of integration which are one of the few counter-forces to rampant nationalism.

We are told that the United States is already entering the "post-industrial society" while half the world has barely begun industrialization. What the implications of this may be are not clear, but it would appear that if we are to help foster industry in the Third World we had better get about it in earnest. It may be that, just as wealth is dividing us ever further from the less developed countries, so our technology may become so sophisticated as to be ever less relevant or useful to those whose economies have not yet entered the twentieth century.

Rather than insisting that the United States is inevitably exploitative and imperialistic, it would be more profitable to examine how we might make our trade and investment more responsive to the needs of the Third World. It is idle to inveigh against the United States as though all trade and investment were evil, without regard for the fact that the Third World wants both and requires both. Private investment overseas can be a potent force for the spread of technology and the process of modernization. It is essential to development in the Third World and is sought after almost everywhere—even where it is also resented. It is a needed complement to economic aid because it can help to bring about the industrialization which all the less developed countries aspire to; to provide jobs and training for those pouring into the cities; to create the opportunities which must be afforded the newly educated; to introduce technology and modern management at no direct cost; to offer a demonstration effect for local groups with enterprise and initiative; to identify areas of economic opportunity based on hard-headed commercial considerations; and to provide essential foreign exchange and tax revenues. It *can* help to do these things; its real contribution is considerably less.

This will surprise no one—least of all those who believe that the profit motive is inherently evil. To these it needs to be said that any expectation of eliminating the desire for gain from the human species does not have very hopeful prospects. Pure communism has been tried repeatedly over many centuries and has not survived more than one or two generations; where it has succeeded briefly it has been on a small scale. The Israeli kibbutz will survive only as long as that country's borders are threatened; as an economic and social organism it is already obsolete. The Communist nations today are permitting small private enterprise and are having to resurrect incentive systems having much in common with "capitalism." And the most rapidly developing societies of today, whether in the industrialized world or the Third World, all have a high quotient of individual enterprise. According to the Peterson Commission,* four fifths of total production in the developing countries comes from the private sector. True, there are a few primitive societies where acquisitiveness is frowned upon and where property is held in common. But what works for a tribe or a village is not necessarily applicable to a modern state. And with remarkably few exceptions, the concepts of capital and profit have been known in the most primitive societies since before recorded history. After the hunter and the farmer came the trader. After bare survival came the accumulation of wealth in the form of cattle or shells or whatever.

This obvious reminder would not be necessary were it not that so many young people are disposed to believe that business is corrupt and corrupting, and to imagine an ideal society in which material wants would be met virtually without effort and no one would have more than was essential—where the

---

* The Peterson Commission was a Presidential task force authorized to make recommendations for the future of foreign aid. It submitted its report early in 1970. See Chapter VIII.

creation of wealth would be unimportant and only its better distribution would matter.

For those who believe that, for all its shortcomings, American business is one of the most creative forces in our society, and that it has an important role to play abroad as well as at home, the concerns are somewhat different. Nevertheless, they are serious. The case against private business abroad can legitimately be built around five points, each one of which deserves more attention than it has received from reformers and protesters:

1. There is a natural but often pernicious tendency for American business abroad to identify the interests of the United States with its own interests. They are not unrelated and they may overlap, but they are by no means the same. The tradition of governments assisting and supporting their citizens in commercial transactions abroad is as old as diplomatic history. But today several new considerations suggest that that assistance and support need to be more qualified. One is the relative importance of political factors in making policy for business as well as governments; the sensitivity of new nations, the fierce nationalism in the Third World, simply do not permit decisions being made on purely economic grounds. If a less developed nation wants to place a reasonable and nondiscriminatory restriction on the amount of profits that can be repatriated in order to increase the amount that is reinvested, the influence of the American government ought not automatically be called upon on behalf of the investor. It may very well be in our larger interest to support the position of the local government. In many of our embassies abroad one frequently encounters tension between the political officers and the commercial attachés, or between the ambassador and the representatives of the American business community. Generally, the former are concerned primarily with maintaining the best possible relations with the host country; the latter are concerned with maximizing profits. The one is not necessarily consistent with the other.

What private companies do or fail to do abroad can involve the reputation and position of the United States very fundamentally. When an American oil company, for example, obstinately resists a reasonable settlement of a claim by a Latin-American country until its investment is angrily nationalized without compensation, the United States government becomes inextricably involved. Obviously we cannot accept confiscation of American property. Yet by all accounts, in the instance referred to, which occurred in 1968, the Standard Oil Company (New Jersey) could and ought to have reached agreement with the Peruvian government long before the issue reached the point of imperiling other U. S. investments, of aggravating already strained relations between the United States and Peru and of stimulating anti-Americanism throughout the hemisphere. Here we see the power of a private company to involve the United States against its will. Jersey Standard, which is the largest foreign investor in the world, believed that a matter of principle was at stake, involving its interests elsewhere. But by its unwillingness to compromise it not only lost its entire investment in Peru, but brought down on itself and other investors the most feared calamity, the worst precedent of all—confiscation. Incidents of this kind, where the United States becomes involved willy-nilly, are not a rare occurrence. The American people ought to be better protected.

2. The sheer size of many American corporations, which is enough to frighten Germans or Frenchmen, can be overwhelming in poor countries. More than half the countries of the world have a GNP which is less than the annual profits of several American corporations. A particular investment which may seem inconsequential to the parent U. S. company may be absolutely vital to the host country. This makes for an inherently unbalanced relationship in which the American company holds most of the chips. In other instances the investment may be very substantial indeed—as in Chile's copper or Saudi Arabia's oil—so that one or two American companies control a very large part of the economy of the host country. In the

developed nations where this is not necessarily the case, U. S. firms may still dominate or control those industrial fields, such as electronics, where some of the most profitable ventures are to be found and where it is difficult to compete without the massive research and development which is a staple of major U. S. corporations.

3. The extensive controls which we have established over private enterprise in the United States often do not exist abroad. Operating in a nineteenth-century commercial environment, with the advantage of the most advanced management and technology, American business presents formidable competition to local industrialists. Many of these, to be sure, are old-time monopolists who resent any competition whatever; in many instances American firms have enormously benefited local consumers by offering better products at lower prices. But the free-wheeling modes of business unknown in the United States for decades still exist abroad, and the temptation to exploit them may be irresistible. Moreover, through ignorance or overeagerness for investment, foreign governments often fail to set those legitimate conditions which will assure that the host nation benefits equally with the American corporation.

4. American business representation abroad is often deplorable. Our businessmen overseas too frequently tend to be of two types: ill-trained but eager young executives, politically illiterate with respect to the country they are serving in, and eager to make their mark and get back to the United States as soon as possible to take the next step up the corporate ladder; and men who have served their whole careers abroad, who have lost touch with the United States and feel much more at home in the country to which they are assigned. They profess to abjure local politics, but in fact have a heavy commitment to whoever is in power; they practice the philosophy of "When in Rome . . ." and they cherish political stability above all other values except profits.

5. What other countries want from foreign private invest-

ment is: economic growth; tax revenues; increased export earn-
ings; some spin-off from the technology involved; work for
their unemployed; training of their nationals to take over an
increasing proportion of technical and managerial positions; a
measure of control; substantial reinvestment of profits; and
opportunity for local investors to obtain an interest in the enterprise. All of these would appear to be legitimate expectations, but only the first two are fulfilled with any consistency.
The other advantages looked for are very unevenly realized.
The technology is often closely held. Many new enterprises are
so highly automated that they actually provide very little employment, though in some fields this is inescapable if the concern is to be competitive. Many American companies are
conscientious about training nationals of the host country to assume greater responsibility, but others do next to nothing.
Some corporations are content if they have fifty-one percent
of the equity or less, while others insist on keeping one hundred
percent. In either case, they generally prefer to make all important decisions in New York or Detroit. With respect to
reinvestment, the record has been uneven, while annual profits
from American enterprises in Asia, Africa and Latin America
have been nearly four times the amount of new investments.
Foreign investors justify high profits on the grounds that political risks are high, thereby aggravating what they most fear.
Finally, very few U. S. corporations permit local investors to
buy shares in their foreign subsidiaries, with the result that for
some nations there is little likelihood of their obtaining adequate control of their own economies.

This indictment would appear to confirm the accusations of
those who charge the United States with economic imperialism,
exploitation of weak states, and domination of the American
government by business. And in some degree it does. But there
are innumerable exceptions to these generalizations, and on
balance the Third World, not to mention Europe and Canada,
has unquestionably benefited from U. S. private investment—
but at a price. Means must now be found to see that the price

is less and the benefit greater without discouraging foreign investment. Many companies have proven that having a conscience, having some concern for the welfare of the country in which it has invested, is not inconsistent with making a satisfactory profit. A prominent New York investment banker has stated the case admirably:

> We pride ourselves on the contribution that large U. S. companies have made through direct investment to economic development in Latin America, Asia and Africa. There is no doubt that they have done much to bring modern methods of production to countries in these areas. But in many, and perhaps in most, instances, the enterprises are managed by Americans and decisions on all major questions are made by the directors in the United States. Too often, the U. S. branches and subsidiaries constitute a sort of technological enclave—foreign-owned, foreign-managed and foreign-directed—in an economy that remains essentially primitive. Is it any wonder that some less developed countries believe that these enterprises have done less than they could or should to foster domestic enterprise, domestic technical development and a broad and balanced industrial economy? . . .
>
> . . . it would be unfortunate if the position of American business abroad were to become dependent on diplomatic pressure from Washington. Ultimately, U. S. companies must adapt themselves to the conditions that confront them abroad; and it would be the highest statesmanship if they took the lead in setting appropriate standards for their operations in foreign countries. First, we must accept the premise that U. S. business—no matter how efficient, no matter how productive—cannot expect to dominate the economy of any country, whether highly industrialized or underdeveloped. Second, we must accept the premise that foreign countries should have access to our technical knowledge without being required to accept domination of their basic industries to acquire it. Third, we must accept the premise that foreign investors, foreign executives and foreign directors have a right to participate in the ownership, management and control of U. S. companies operating in their countries.

Once these premises are accepted, the practical solution becomes evident. No U. S. company should control all or nearly all of a basic industry in a foreign country if any part of the business can be done by local firms. Instead of shutting out competition, our companies should help to establish it. Whenever strategic considerations do not prevent it, U. S. companies should enter into licensing agreements for the use of their patents and technical processes by domestic companies in the countries in which they operate. Such a policy is, after all, much the same as they are required to follow in the United States under the antitrust laws. . . .

Finally, U. S. companies abroad should conduct their operations in complete harmony with the political, economic and social objectives of the host country. For the U. S. Government this would require a self-denying policy on the use of the Trading with the Enemy Act to control the operations of foreign branches and subsidiaries, except in time of emergency. For U. S. companies, this would require that some of the principal executive officers and directors be nationals of the host country. The participation of foreign nationals in management and control should be more than nominal. It would defeat the purpose of such a policy if the officers and directors of a foreign subsidiary were no more than local agents carrying out directives from the head office in the United States.*

American business is not more culpable than that of other countries, but it generally weighs more heavily in the affairs of other nations. And since the emergence of the U. S. balance-of-payments problem, the American government has aggravated the situation by restricting dollar investments abroad and encouraging repatriation of profits rather than reinvestment. This is but one way in which Washington exerts control over foreign subsidiaries that appears negative from the standpoints of both American business and the host country. Others are application of our anti-trust laws and of the Trading with the Enemy Act, whereby foreign subsidiaries are precluded—just as are domes-

* Leo Model, "The Politics of Foreign Investment," *Foreign Affairs,* July 1967, pp. 647-51.

tic firms—from trading with specified countries. These modern forms of extraterritoriality cause far more resentment than their value to us warrants; none has been particularly successful in achieving its objectives, and the sooner they are dropped the better.

Yet most governments give more favorable treatment to their own foreign traders and investors—through tax provisions, credit guarantees and diplomatic influence—than does the United States. All governments exert some control over their business concerns operating abroad, and until some international institution is created to assume this responsibility, one would hardly want it otherwise. Many suggestions are currently being made for codes of behavior or international regulation or courts of arbitration which would set ground rules for the so-called multinational corporation. It will be difficult to win acceptance of any of these, but each has merit. Though no definition of the multinational corporation has won acceptance, it is instructive to know that there are more than 600 companies with operations in ten or more foreign countries; there are perhaps 200 companies having 25 percent or more of their operations abroad, as measured by profits, assets, employment or sales (excluding exports). They have an enormous potential for creating a real international community. But if they are to become truly international, they must operate by a single set of rules which will ensure fair competition and fair treatment; and they must be freed of the undue influence of national governments.

Until that time arrives, one can hope that American companies and the U. S. government will impose voluntary restraints on themselves and show a more lively concern for the interests of host countries in the less developed world. As part of U. S. technical assistance we might counsel foreign governments negotiating with American corporations, advising them as to what they are entitled to demand. If we are serious about the welfare of the new nations, then we are entitled to protect them in the same way that government protects vulnerable groups and individuals at home. Whatever the formula, it is becoming increasingly apparent that the U. S. government and the people it represents are entitled to make some demands on American companies operating abroad, in return for a measure of protection and assistance. Although there is informal consultation between government and business on issues involving the national interest, it takes place in Washington, not in the field where Foreign Service officers and American businessmen too often share a mutual antagonism, even contempt. Although companies do not make a practice of defying the government's wishes, in the last analysis they are free to complicate and damage our diplomacy as it may appear to serve their interests.

As a start toward achieving a set of standards for business practices abroad, the new Overseas Private Investment Corporation (OPIC), recently authorized by Congress, might be a useful instrument. Voluntary acceptance of some limitations would be preferable to government regulation, though one cannot be very hopeful that American business will surrender its freedom of action voluntarily. Nevertheless, OPIC might do much to show American firms "how to make their investments more acceptable to the host country," in the words of the Peterson Commission report. In particular it ought to consider the many methods suggested for transferring ownership of American enterprises to the host countries, so that we are not forever exposed to the charge of neocolonialism.* It ought to be made clear that if American business abroad is not more responsive to the demands of the host countries and the broad interests of the United States, then government regulation will, and ought to, follow.

Those who are inclined to believe that foreign investment represents a net loss to the less developed world should re-

* See, for example, Albert O. Hirschman, *How to Divest in Latin America, and Why,* Essays in International Finance, No. 76, Princeton University, November 1969; and Paul Streeten, "Obstacles to Private Foreign Investment in the LDCs," *Columbia Journal of World Business,* May–June 1970.

member that the growth of the United States in the nineteenth century and after would have been impossible without the use of European capital. The difference is that because we had great natural wealth and adequate managerial and technical skills, we were able to borrow money, generally in the form of bond issues, without losing control of the enterprise. This lack in today's less developed countries is being met by various international banking institutions created expressly to meet the needs of the Third World, which often cannot borrow from commercial banks in the West, either because the risks seem too high or because they cannot afford the interest charges. Yet the needs are so vast that every means has a part to play in the developmental process: grants, official loans and credits, bank loans at concessional rates, commercial loans and private investment. Each complements the others.

The capacities and creativity of American enterprise are so enormous that ways must be found to use them more effectively in economic development without exposing us to charges of economic imperialism. In some instances it should be possible to persuade American corporations to launch a new enterprise abroad with the understanding that after, say, ten years of profit-taking, ownership would revert to the host government or its people through the sale of stock, with the possibility that the enterprise might continue to be operated by the American corporation on a fee basis for an additional period if necessary. The objection offered is that, without a continuing interest, the American corporation would bleed the enterprise white during its decade of ownership and leave it a shambles. This is a danger that surely can be overcome by reasonable and acceptable controls and the need of the parent company to preserve its reputation in the host country.

There is an array of arrangements whereby foreign investors can make a profit and at the same time not only benefit the host country, but give it some sense of control. American corporations are increasingly realizing that they can afford to share ownership of their subsidiaries and are therefore going into joint ventures with the host country. There are co-production agreements under which ownership accrues to the host country and the foreigner is paid off in kind; and so-called turnkey arrangements, whereby, for a fixed fee, a foreign firm builds a plant, trains workers and managers, and then turns the whole operation over to the host government. Many American companies have found it advantageous to enter into technical assistance and operations contracts, even where the profits were not high. For example, TWA has been operating Ethiopian Airlines for a fee of $35,000 a year and trying to do itself out of the job as soon as possible by training managers, pilots, engineers, and repair and maintenance workers. The benefit to Ethiopia has been enormous: a profitable airline (almost unheard of in Africa) and the first nationwide transportation system that that mountainous country has ever had. The benefit to TWA has been confined to building good will in Africa and stimulating air traffic which feeds into TWA's network of international flights.

Whether or not adequate solutions can be found, these facts remain and must be coped with: (a) the Third World needs and wants the initiative, skills and capital of American private enterprise; (b) America's influence and reputation in the world is shaped importantly by the performance of American business abroad; and (c) both the United States and the less developed countries need protection from abuse of power by U. S. corporations operating overseas.

The United States has no need or desire to dominate the world—economically or otherwise. If domination had been its objective, we would not have overlooked so many ways to exploit the dependence of others upon us. We would not have sought to build areas of strength in Europe, Asia and Latin America. We would not repeatedly have helped Britain out of its financial crises and France out of its colonial crises. We would not have withdrawn from areas of military involvement in Africa, Latin America and the Middle East, nor urged our allies to maintain a presence in regions of historical concern.

We would not have urged self-determination and independence for the scores of new nations that have emerged in recent decades—or, having done so, we would have seized the opportunity to achieve predominance among them. In the relatively few instances where the former colonial powers are no longer the dominant external force in the territories they once administered, it is generally the Soviet Union which has replaced them—not the United States.

Without over-all plan or intent, nevertheless, American business interests have reached out to play a significant role in the economies—and inescapably the politics—of many countries. If serious friction is to be avoided, greater restraint and responsibility will be required. Above all, the less developed countries must feel that decisions affecting their destiny are within their control. Conversely, as long as individual corporations can drag this country into situations of acute discomfort or peril, as long as they fail to be responsive to the justified demands of the host countries, American foreign policy will be compromised. Here lies a verdant field for protest and reform.

VIII

Aid's Summer Soldiers

No ASPECT of foreign policy has been so exhaustively studied and eloquently defended as foreign economic aid. In a six-month period of 1969–70 no less than five major national and international reports on economic development and foreign aid were published* without visible effect on public or Congressional opinion in the United States. At a time when other nations, including beleaguered Britain, are increasing their foreign aid by 5 to 10 percent per year, ours has been declining by about the same amount. Moreover, this is occurring at a time when the capacity of less developed countries to use capital effectively is increasing, and when they are being more serious

* (1) The Commission on International Development, which was sponsored by the World Bank and headed by Lester Pearson, and whose comprehensive report was published in the autumn of 1969 (by Praeger) under the title *Partners in Development;* (2) the Presidential Task Force on International Development, headed by Rudolph A. Peterson, which submitted its report in March 1970; (3) the U. N. Committee on Development Planning, under Professor Jan Tinbergen, which set out guidelines for the Second United Nations Development Decade; (4) the study of the United Nations Development System carried out by Sir Robert Jackson; (5) the Rockefeller Report on Latin America. In addition, there was the report of the President's General Advisory Committee on Foreign Assistance Problems (James A. Perkins, chairman) in October 1968, and two private independent studies in 1969 by the National Planning Association and the Committee for Economic Development.

about their own efforts—in short, when our dollars could be used more efficiently.

It seems strange that those who are most critical of American foreign policy and who are articulate about the importance of morality in international relations have paid so little attention to these circumstances. No doubt it is partly due to a legitimate concern for our domestic needs and a conviction that our priorities should be altered. But it also arises from a variety of misconceptions which can be placed on a political spectrum.

On the far left are those who oppose economic aid not through any misunderstanding, but because they believe it might delay the revolutions which they hope will occur throughout the Third World. This backhanded compliment to the possible efficacy of foreign aid merely needs recording.

Another faction holds that, since American society is hopelessly corrupted, it must corrupt whatever it touches; therefore, hands off the as yet unsullied societies of Asia and Africa! Let them follow their own way, adhere to their own values. We have nothing to give except our materialism and our own distorted sense of values.

This strange recrudescence of the "noble savage" theory, which one had thought was long dead, cannot seriously be held by anyone who has traveled in less developed countries. For whatever disenchanted Americans may think of the results of technology and mass production, the people of the Third World wants its benefits. Their leaders are aware that their careers, their very lives, may depend on achieving visible economic growth. To romanticize man in a state of nature is to betray an ignorance of nature's cruelty and of the extent to which peoples everywhere aspire to what they now know exists and is at least theoretically attainable.

We are talking about a world where the gap between the rich nations and the poor nations is in the ratio of 15 to 1 and widening steadily. It is a world in which illiteracy is increasing despite the high value that is placed on education in the developing nations. It is a world in which a couple may have to have five children to assure (statistically) that one will reach the age of fifteen. It is a world in which probably half of the children are suffering from some degree of malnutrition. The result is that not only are they fatally susceptible to infectious diseases, but their intelligence is often permanently affected, their mental development stunted. Is this the romantic world which some would have us leave to its own devices?

Improved nutrition may well be the nearest thing we have to a key to the problem of development. It would improve the effectiveness of birth-control efforts by convincing parents that it is not necessary to have eight or ten children in order to have two survivors to support them in their old age. It would raise the productivity of workers and extend their productive years. It would vastly reduce the costs of medical care by reducing susceptibility to disease and eliminating diseases—beriberi, certain forms of blindness—which are attributable to malnutrition. These things are measurable; the psychic gains are incalculable. Moreover, we already have the technology to eliminate malnutrition at surprisingly low costs, though problems of distributing protein-enriched foods and of altering people's eating habits remain.

For those looking for a purpose, surely here is one. The solution is not, as some think, for the United States to go on making up food deficits abroad. Between 1954 and the end of 1966 we shipped some $15.7 billion worth of food overseas on concessional terms and were feeding more than 160 million people abroad.* As a stopgap measure it was mutually advantageous, but it is not a healthy situation to have countries so dependent on us as, for example, India has been in this regard. Also, our massive food shipments permitted the Indians to postpone coming to grips with their agricultural problems, which have only recently received the priority they deserved. Ultimately we must help other regions to become more nearly

* Orville L. Freeman, "Malthus, Marx and the North American Bread-basket," *Foreign Affairs,* July 1967, p. 592.

self-sufficient in basic foods. Before World War II, only Western Europe was a net importer of grain. Now Latin America, which had been the largest exporter, is barely self-sufficient and all other areas except North America and Australia are net importers. Grain exports from the United States have increased 1,200 percent in the postwar period.

Unfortunately, for most of the world's hungry it is the volume of food in the belly that counts, not the nutritional value. In Java, for example, land-poor farmers will plant cassava instead of rice (though they prefer the latter) because its bulk goes further to still the hunger pains, but it is even more deficient in protein than rice.

What is valued after food and education and perhaps health care is things. Some of the critics of whom we have been speaking would deny that man is an acquisitive animal and assert that demand is being artificially created in order to promote sales of what is not needed. Others who have observed the Third World at closer range would agree that all people who have been even brushed by world civilization are remarkably materialistic. An Asian has written: "Asians are materialistic and they want a better standard of living. If they appear to be more non-materialistic or appear to be needing less or appear to be fatalistic, these are only manifestations of a defense mechanism to defend their high expectations."* And so it is in every other continent. "All those resigned people" of whom André Gide wrote in his *Travels in the Congo* are largely gone. No longer do they "stagnate in a sort of precarious felicity, incapable, no doubt, of even imagining a better state of things." By the millions they are drifting away from the land and toward nonexistent opportunities in the cities, where their desires are inflamed as their expectations are frustrated.

To be sure, Africans and Asians hope to achieve the best of both worlds—to graft our skills and technology onto their own cultures without loss of their own identity or the aspects of life they wish to preserve. Perhaps they will achieve a new syn-

* Paul Sithi-Amnuai, "The Asian Mind," *Asia,* Spring 1968, p. 90.

thesis of sorts; probably, they will acquire more of the negative aspects of Western civilization than they expect. But without exception they are prepared to run that risk, for they have no alternative. They cannot go back; their isolation is long since ended. They can go forward at adequate rates of development only with the help of those with advanced technologies. The view that we will be doing them a favor by withholding what they most want, and most keenly resent the absence of, seems to them the very height of hypocrisy.

Surely on this point we may believe Frantz Fanon. Though he admonished the Third World not to imitate Europe, he believed that aid from the industrialized world was of crucial importance. He demanded it as "just reparation" for past plundering. "Europe," he wrote, "is literally the creation of the Third World. The wealth which smothers her is that which was stolen from the underdeveloped peoples."* This latter point is, of course, largely untrue. If real wealth were created in this way, then the Turks, the Persians and the Arabs would be the equal of Europe, China would be far ahead of Japan, and Spain would be the wealthiest of European countries. Most of the plundering was done in areas which have been independent longest, and in much of the Third World the colonial powers gave as much as or more than they took. Nevertheless, the concept of "just reparation" is not without some validity, not so much because of wealth "stolen" as because of other injustices, including the psychic damage of subjugation.

Related to the previous objection to foreign aid is the notion that it is merely a form of neocolonialism. It is a foot in the door which will be pushed open by foreign capitalist exploiters. The only beneficiary of foreign aid is American business.

Here there is at least a kernel of truth, but a small one. It is given some credence in the less developed countries themselves. Nkrumah cultivated this argument to full flower, but

---

* Fanon, *The Wretched of the Earth* (New York: Grove Press, Evergreen paperback edition), p. 102.

never ceased to demand more of both public aid and private capital. However, there is no inevitable connection between official foreign aid and private investment. Any country is free to admit one without the other, although it is true we have sometimes argued that a particular project could be carried out better by private means and that public aid should be preserved for projects which will not attract private capital.

The most immediate U. S. benefit from aid is that most of the loans and grants are spent in this country. Moreover, for the past several years aid loans have been "tied" (except recently in Latin America)—that is, our aid dollars *must* be spent in the United States (which nevertheless has said it is willing to drop tied loans if the other lending nations agree to do so). Thus about eighty cents of every dollar of economic aid returns to this country in the form of orders for earth movers, tractors, railroad engines or whatever. When it is further considered that the greater part of American aid is now in the form of loans rather than grants and that increasing rates of interest are charged, it is certainly less than true to say that our aid program is "a giveaway."

It is sad, however, to see the radical left seizing arguments employed to persuade Congress that aid is of some benefit to us and using them to assert that aid has benefited only the donor countries. It is now being contended that aid as well as investment is a device of the industrialized nations to penetrate and ultimately to control the Third World. And now that the United States appears more willing to give through multilateral institutions, these are condemned as even more insidious instruments, in that they will reduce the bargaining power of the less developed nations. Multilateralism is seen by some as an international conspiracy to dictate terms on which the developed countries will exploit the markets and natural resources of the Third World. This will be fostered by the fact that "most Third World countries are run by neo-colonial elites who are neither representative of their own people nor committed to more than their own aggrandizement."* Thus both sides are damned and there is apparently no alternative but bloody revolution. Even then, these critics do not indicate how the Third World is to go forward on any scale of progress they may wish to define without substantial transfers of wealth in some form. They forget, perhaps, that Castro's much admired revolution has been costing the Soviet Union about a million dollars a day for more than a decade.

Another facet of this general view is that foreign aid is merely a way of buying client states. Intended as a condemnation of American policy, this contention is both an insult to the receiving nations and a far departure from reality. It should by now be clear to the American public, as it has long been clear to government officials, that it is very hard to buy even the good will, much less the unquestioned loyalty, of other nations. Perhaps only Congress supposed this was ever possible and it has been punishing AID (Agency for International Development) ever since it found this was not to be one of the benefits of economic aid.

Nevertheless, as the Peterson Commission report emphasizes, a distinction should be made between economic aid (development loans and technical assistance) and security assistance—the latter having three categories: military aid; what has been called "support assistance" (for countries like Korea and Turkey which maintain abnormally large armies); and emergency grants to countries in crisis. No doubt some of those who have received security assistance have felt heavily dependent on us, but this has arisen not from the fact of our aid but from the inherent situation in which they found themselves. In this sense it may be defensible to call South Korea, for instance, a client state, though it is certainly tactless. But to extend the term to all countries to which we have given economic aid is to be heedless of the strength of national pride.

It is true that in the late fifties and early sixties, less devel-

* *International Dependency in the 1970's,* prepared by the Africa Research Group, Cambridge, Mass. (mimeographed), pp. 15-16.

oped nations talked a lot about "strings" being attached to aid, but they gradually learned that these were not demands for conformity to our political views but were legitimate requirements relating to such things as tax collection, restraints on consumption and control of inflation. This much surely the American taxpayer has every right to expect—namely, that the receiving nation demonstrate its good faith and seriousness about economic development.

No doubt this is not the whole story. We did not always accept neutralism and nonalignment and often became irritated with countries which professed neutrality but did not appear in our judgment to practice it. This, however, has been a declining problem since the fifties. Also, we have suspended aid when a constitutional government was overthrown by left or right; hence resumption of aid could inescapably be interpreted as a political reward for returning to the proper path. In fact our motives are rarely so simple. In 1969 we cut off $180 million of aid to Brazil to show our displeasure with the repressions of its military regime. We resumed aid in 1970 not because the situation had improved or because we were taking a more tolerant view of totalitarianism, but because on reflection it was decided that this was not an effective or sensible means of registering disapproval. Economic development is a long-term effort designed to help people, not regimes. If we turn off a major source of capital every time there is a military coup in Latin America, progress will be nearly impossible. Unfortunately, it is also true that, as compared to more democratic governments, military regimes often do a better job of administering development plans, because they have the political power to make tough and often unpopular decisions. In the case of Brazil, some of its economic policies have been startlingly progressive. For example, the junta has launched a plan whereby workers will receive a percentage of corporate sales. It is said that within four years workers will benefit to the extent of $1 billion.

Similarly, we cut off aid to Sukarno's Indonesia not because he was undemocratic or overly tolerant of Communism (both true and evident for a long time), but because he was not serious about economic development and was scandalously wasteful of his country's resources. Indonesia still has an undemocratic regime, but we are giving substantial assistance because it has shown a determination to create those conditions in which economic development is possible. That it is also anti-Communist is no doubt a factor in its favor, especially before Congressional committees, but among responsible officials who are serious about development it is a secondary consideration.

Examples could be multiplied. The point is that by and large we have not used economic development aid merely to further our own special interests, and most leaders of the Third World have come to acknowledge this. It would be reckless to assert that we have never used our economic leverage with other countries. Diplomacy is the art of persuasion, and on any day around the world our representatives are trying to persuade nations—those to whom we grant aid and those we don't—to change course or adopt particular policies, as others equally try to persuade us. Whether those who receive our aid are more susceptible to persuasion is a moot point; the record is certainly not conclusive. In any event, the recommendation of the Peterson Commission that we give a higher proportion of our aid through multilateral organizations seems likely to be followed, thereby further reducing the danger of our exercising unwarranted influence on recipient countries. Moreover, the President's task force urges that in that part of our aid which remains bilateral we follow the lead of the multilateral institutions, fitting our program into theirs.

Oddly, those who believe most firmly that we attach unacceptable strings to our aid would be most outraged if, without exception, we had none. Chiang Kai-shek has been restrained from adventures on the mainland by the certain knowledge that they would lead to a suspension of aid (though he now receives no economic aid and needs none). Similarly, one of our few weapons in avoiding war between Greece and Turkey in 1968 was the threat of cutting off all forms of aid to an aggressor. If this is a price that aid receivers pay for American assistance, the world is surely the better for it.

Skeptics will not be reassured by words alone. Nevertheless, it is significant that the Peterson Commission report, which may be adopted as official policy in principle if not in detail, is categorical in rejecting some of the illusions of the past:

> This country should not look for gratitude or votes, or any specific short-term foreign policy gains from our participation in international development. Nor should it expect to influence others to adopt U. S. cultural values or institutions. Neither can it assume that development will necessarily bring political stability. Development implies change—political and social, as well as economic—and such change, for a time, may be disruptive.*

Again, closely allied to the foregoing criticism is the assertion that we use economic aid to prop up unpopular dictatorships. This accusation has in part been answered; in Latin America our aid cannot be effective if we help only democracies or if we cut off aid after every coup. Indeed, it is probably true that the only hope of ending the cycle of coup and countercoup in Latin America is through a concerted effort at economic development which will inescapably bring with it social and political change. It is significant that many of the eminent democrats of Latin America do not share the widespread abhorrence of aiding dictatorships. For example, Galo Plaza, one of the most respected of international statesmen and a former President of Ecuador, recently made a study of Haiti, generally considered to be the most oppressive and unenlightened dictatorship in all of Latin America and a country which the United States had long since ceased to aid. He concluded that

* Letter to President Nixon from the sixteen-member task force headed by Rudolph A. Peterson, printed in *The New York Times,* March 9, 1970. The letter also appears as an introduction to the report, *U. S. Foreign Assistance in the 1970s: A New Approach* (Washington: G.P.O., March 4, 1970), p. 2.

foreign aid would neither strengthen nor weaken President Duvalier, but that it would do some good for the miserable Haitian people. Galo Plaza urged the United States to resume aid. Washington replied, quite understandably, that a direct aid program was politically impossible. It was finally agreed, however, that we would provide limited funds for this purpose through the Organization of American States, which meant that the Latins themselves assumed responsibility for aiding Haiti.

Another complaint against foreign aid has been that we have underestimated the social and political factors in development and have mistakenly assumed that capital transfers were sufficient. Strangely, this argument often comes from those who believe we have interfered too much in the affairs of other nations. What, then, are we to do? Wash our hands of the problem entirely? It is true that there is a great deal about the development process that we do not understand; there are also things we understand and can do little about. But if anyone supposed that economic development was a purely mechanistic phenomenon, in which certain economic inputs would bring certain results, he has long since learned otherwise. The importance of cultural factors, social organization, structural reform, motivation, adaptability and the like is adequately appreciated, at least in the United States, if not fully understood. It is a fascinating question why, for example, Japan has emerged as the third industrial power in the world, while China—with so many cultural similarities, far richer in resources and with an equally energetic people—should still be floundering. Clearly it is not explained by the Communist–capitalist dichotomy alone.

To a degree we have reacted to this accusation of neglecting social and political factors by increasingly concentrating our aid on a very few nations where over-all conditions for economic development seem most propitious. We are now providing significant assistance only to some fifteen countries, which means that the vast majority are being neglected—at least by the United States. This may be justified on the grounds that, with limited resources, it is necessary to concentrate our effort in order to achieve a significant impact. Also, the demonstration effect of a few countries emerging into genuine economic independence would probably have a more beneficial effect on all of the Third World than a more equitable distribution of aid. Moreover, the tragic fact is that for at least several score countries economic independence with a tolerable standard of life seems unattainable as far as the eye can see. But to oppose foreign aid on the grounds that we do not understand—or cannot control—the political, social and cultural factors affecting development is rather like opposing civil-rights efforts because we do not know how to eradicate prejudice.

One of the illusions that has hurt foreign aid is that it leads to military involvement. There is simply no basis for this assumption. We did not become involved in Vietnam out of any economic interest whatever. Three of our largest aid programs are in India, Nigeria and Brazil, with whom we have no special defense relationships. No country has been more jealous of its neutrality than India. In the case of Nigeria, we were one of the few major powers to remain uninvolved in its civil war. Our defense relationship with Taiwan and our military involvement with Korea preceded our economic-aid programs. Ending economic aid to Taiwan has not ended our defense arrangements. Similarly, we have been phasing out economic aid to Turkey without any intention of altering our treaty arrangements which exist through NATO. In brief, no demonstrable link exists between economic aid and military involvement.

Probably the largest body of complaints is that foreign aid has been wasteful, badly administered, and ineffectively used by the recipients. What, it is asked, do we have to show for our money? If, after so much effort, the poor are getting poorer as the rich are getting richer, what can we do about it but leave them to their own devices? Our resources are finite and the wants of the underdeveloped world are insatiable.

This attitude stems in part from the fact that economic aid

was oversold. Too much was expected in too short a time. Some of the developmental economists were themselves too optimistic in the early days when we were shifting our aid from Europe, where accomplishment had been spectacular, to the less developed world, which had neither the skills nor the infrastructure (roads, electric power, etc.) for rapid growth. The need to "sell" foreign aid to Congress every year led to exaggerated claims. Annually, the aid bill had to be pushed through no fewer than eight Congressional committees, and year by year as resistance stiffened the temptation of officials to claim more for foreign aid than could be delivered was irresistible. No major undertaking of the United States at home or abroad ever had to fight for its life so often or so strenuously.

Moreover, there were reorganizations and changes in emphasis every few years, based partly on better understanding of the requirements and processes of development, but more often for essentially irrational reasons arising from political pressures. No doubt money was and still is being wasted. We were entering a new field; there was a scatteration of effort; political and social restraints on economic development were underestimated and insufficiently understood; we were working in and with societies of which we knew little and trying to overcome forms of resistance which were baffling. Most important, a relatively small proportion of aid was actually applied to economic development, as opposed to military and support aid, import credits, food programs, making up operating deficits, refinancing loans or assisting in the control of inflation.

The body of experience we have accumulated over the past decade or more offers some considerable promise for the long-range future. Not only have we learned, but, more important, the less developed countries themselves have learned not only that there are no quick solutions but that they must be serious in their efforts. The day of grandiloquent schemes designed to make a political impact or satisfy the vanity of politicians is largely over—and to our credit we did not indulge in them to the extent that other donor nations did. The importance of agriculture and the need for fiscal responsibility is better recognized. Suspicion of foreign advisers has somewhat eased at the same time that their fallibility has become better recognized. In many of the less developed countries there is now a small but competent staff of trained economists and technicians capable of making informed decisions and using aid effectively. Some countries have made no distinguishable progress in the past decade; indeed, several have retrogressed. A few have achieved remarkable rates of growth, while others have reached a point at which more rapid progress can be expected in coming decades if reasonably adequate capital is made available.

There are additional reasons for the increased absorptive capacity, as it is called, of the developing nations. One of special importance is the new seed, especially rice and corn, which holds out so much promise for easing the world food shortage. Countries which have not been self-sufficient in food for generations are approaching or surpassing that point. But these seeds require large investments of fertilizer and pesticides and create heavier demands for irrigation. Hence the opportunities for foreign aid to provide a tangible return were never so favorable.

It is not true, then, that foreign aid has accomplished nothing or that the demands of the Third World are insatiable. Progress has been very uneven, and per-capita rates of growth have been adversely affected almost everywhere by fearsome increases in population. Indeed, one of the reasons the advanced nations have a continuing obligation to the Third World is that, having been largely responsible for the population explosion through the eradication of disease and improved medical care, we cannot now abandon the developing countries to face the resulting problem alone. Of course, we too have an interest in curbing birth rates, for we all share one planet of finite size and resources. And it is obvious to almost everyone that satisfactory rates of economic growth cannot be achieved where population growth devours the greater part of any gains. It is sad to hear American radicals mimicking the groundless charge of demagogues abroad that birth control is a device for keeping less developed countries small and weak. China's vast population is not an asset but a liability; there are simply too many mouths to feed, and precious foreign exchange has had to be used to buy food abroad. The development of Brazil's untapped interior is being delayed not by an insufficiency of people, but by an insufficiency of capital and motivation. Meanwhile the slums radiate ever farther outward from cities seething with the discontents of the unemployed and children who cannot be adequately cared for.

Most studies have agreed that aid to the Third World, from all sources, public and private, will need to be doubled in the next few years if the potential for development is to be realized. That is to say, the Third World can effectively and efficiently use on the order of $16 billion a year in this decade. This is less than Americans alone contribute to charitable purposes annually.

Sixteen billion dollars is not an impossible figure for the developed world to sustain. With modest growth in private investment, it could be achieved if the developed countries gave somewhat less than the 1 percent of GNP which has been a goal long urged in the United Nations. The United States is far from that goal and slipping by about 10 percent a year while a majority of the developed nations are increasing their contribution. Even some of our most liberal Senators are now opponents of aid, and for reasons which are not confined to the priority which domestic problems deserve. Hardly anyone would contest this, but the two goals are not mutually exclusive. The notion that we must do less abroad because we must do more at home stems in part from an illusion that we can buy our way out of our domestic problems. But money alone won't solve our difficulties at home any more than it has done so abroad. For some, the war in Vietnam is an excuse to do less, forgetting that we fought the Korean War while giving 3 percent of our GNP in Marshall Plan aid; we are now down to between .33 and .6 percent, depending upon how "aid" is calculated. In these terms, the United States, which contains 6 percent of the world's population but consumes nearly 40 percent of the world's resources, ranks eleventh among aid-giving nations.*

Moreover, grants have been declining even more rapidly than total aid, which means that loans—generally in the form of import credits—are proportionately increasing. And the terms of these loans—their duration and the rates of interest paid—are becoming markedly stiffer, which aggravates the already staggering burden of debt service. According to the Pearson Commission report, repayment of previous loans (principal and interest) by Latin America amounts to 87 percent of new loans, and by present projections the figure will soon be over 100 percent. The comparable figure for Africa is 73 percent, while Asia's is somewhat lower.† These figures are so high not because aid has been so great, but because a large part of the borrowing has been in the form of supplier credits at high rates of interest and very short term. As the greater part of the new aid loans are likely to be in the form of import credits, they cannot be used to service old debts; for this, hard-currency foreign exchange must be found. For some countries more than 25 percent of export income must be used for debt service.

To be sure, not all the less developed countries are heavily in debt, and the nearly impossible burdens that some carry are

---

* The illusion persists that it is abnormal to spend more than a minute proportion of our budget on the conduct of international relations in all its facets. Yet in 1793 Congress appropriated between 10 and 20 percent of the budget for foreign affairs, entirely apart from defense; see Henry Wriston, *Diplomacy in a Democracy* (New York: Harper, 1956), pp. 28-29. In the entire postwar period in which we have been alleged to be overinvolved, we have not come close to the lower figure, and today virtually every aspect of our representation abroad is being drastically cut back. Cultural and educational exchanges have been reduced to a third of what they were a few years ago. At times, the State Department budget has been so tight that American ambassadors have not been able to travel within their own region or to see other U. S. envoys in the same area.

† *Partners in Development,* p. 74.

often of their own making. Nevertheless, virtually all students of economic development agree not only that aid must be substantially increased, but that much of it must be in long-term loans at rates of interest very much below commercial levels.

One of many points on which all major studies agree is that aid-giving should be increasingly multilateral. For the recipient nations this has the advantage of reducing the dangers of political pressure; for the donors there is the advantage of sharing responsibility and possibly of having their advice more readily accepted. International financial institutions such as the World Bank and its affiliates, and regional banks, now provide more than half of all development loans. Although there is still some resistance to multilateralism in the United States, as elsewhere, the variety of available institutions makes it more attractive to donor nations than when the United Nations was almost alone in the field. If this seems an unwarranted reflection on the U. N., it is no more than has been said in the report of a study which the U. N. itself commissioned. The Jackson Report questions the capacity of the U. N. Development Program effectively to double its present outlays, which are now a modest $200 million, unless its methods are radically revamped. On the basis of an extended study, the Jackson Report found the U. N. overburdened, clumsy and slow, and its effectiveness limited by rivalries and lack of coordination among its various agencies. Morale in the Secretariat is low.

Even with greater efficiency in the U. N. system, it cannot be assumed that aid received through the U. N. shields the recipient nation from all unwarranted pressures. The U. N. is a highly politicized organization and subject to its own pressures arising from the enormous variety in its membership. The point of this is not to derogate the work of the U. N., but to suggest that it ought not to be overburdened.

There is a somewhat similar danger of expecting too much of the World Bank. It made its excellent reputation originally by the thoroughness of its investigations of projects and the high standards it set in making loans. It concentrated on projects which were economically sound and on which the financial payoff would be prompt. The Bank is now being asked—and under Mr. McNamara is willingly accepting—to do much more. It is becoming deeply involved in the economies of particular countries and is assuming heavy responsibilities for achieving progress. Where expectations are not fulfilled, the Bank may begin to draw the fire previously aimed at AID. By subcontracting much of its work to private concerns in a variety of countries, the Bank may avoid the kind of bureaucracy from which AID has suffered, yet the rapid growth of its resources and operations, which are now bigger than AID's, will almost inescapably bring some dilution of quality.

We need not dwell here on the criticisms of foreign aid that come from the right: that it is a gigantic steal from the American taxpayer; that it is money down a rathole; that it serves only to promote world socialism. These chestnuts have been around from the beginning of the aid program and can be resisted in the future as they have been in the past. What is troubling is that so many liberals, and now leftists, are throwing their lot with unreconstructed critics of the right—ceasing to be constructively critical and often putting themselves in outright opposition. There have been many mistakes in our aid programs—mistakes of emphasis, administration, purpose, style and salesmanship. But most have been honest mistakes made in a pioneering effort where we were feeling our way. A lot of idealism has gone into the undertaking, and it would be tragic to abandon it now.

One of the most experienced and respected developmental economists, John P. Lewis, has put the case this way (in a letter to the Peterson task force):

> To assert the abiding national interest of the U. S. in seeking sufficient economic acceleration in the poor countries to commence a reliable, if gradual, convergence of the income gaps is not to assume that growth rates and "political stability" are

neatly or simply correlated—nor is it to say that economic performance is a sufficient index of the human condition. It is only to place a wager: that in a turbulent, development-bent world already irreversibly infected with an appetite for radical social and economic change, faster economic growth is *likely* to be a lubricant of change; in general, it is apt to facilitate more humane outcomes, more constructive social experiments, less contentious reorderings of income distributions and status structures, more open-endedness in political procedures, and less disruptive behavior internationally than will the frustrations of aspiring but stagnant economies.

The Pearson Commission report argues even more eloquently:

> Concern with the needs of other and poorer nations is the expression of a new and fundamental aspect of the modern age—the awareness that we live in a village world, that we belong to a world community.
>
> It is this which makes the desire to help into more than a moral impulse felt by an individual; makes it into a political and social imperative for governments, which now accept at least a degree of accountability in their relations with each other.
>
> . . . Who can now ask where his country will be in a few decades without asking where the world will be? If we wish that world to be secure and prosperous, we must show a common concern for the common problems of all people.*

One wishes that young people, especially, could sufficiently curb their cynicism about government and the aims of the United States to release that natural idealism which they demonstrate at home and which is urgently called for abroad. The cause of foreign developmental aid needs all the friends it can get.

* *Partners in Development*, pp. 8-9.

IX

Anatomy of
Two Dilemmas

THE PROBLEM OF ARMS SALES AND AID

THAT THE United States is the world's largest supplier of arms
—some $67 billion worth since World War II—is used as
prima-facie evidence that we are not seriously interested in
peace and in fact promote wars. How can we profess to be
concerned about arms control and military expenditures
throughout the world, and at the same time provide arms to
some eighty nations? Apparently we do not gain significant
influence, for, on the testimony of the Secretary of State, not
a single instance can be cited of success in altering the policies
of a country by withholding military aid where it had previously been provided. Especially deplorable is the diversion of
funds urgently needed for development. Although military expenditures in the developed world are declining in real terms,
according to the U. S. Arms Control and Disarmament
Agency, they are increasing rapidly in the less developed
world—about 11 percent a year over the past six years,
despite generally insignificant rates of economic growth.
Ninety-three less developed countries as a group are spending
more on military budgets than on education and public health

combined.* Thoughtful Americans, including members of Congress, are rightly disturbed, and many take the attitude that military aid and sales should be stopped everywhere and at once. Unhappily, this would not do even our consciences much good.

First, some background. Overwhelmingly the largest part of our military aid has gone to countries on the Sino–Soviet periphery—the NATO countries, Korea, Taiwan, South Vietnam—and apart from Indochina it is declining rapidly. Another portion, also declining, was a *quid pro quo* for base rights—Spain, Pakistan and Ethiopia are examples—some of which we have given up. As recently as 1962, 97 percent of arms sales went to the developed world, the only area in which we have indulged in "hard sell." However, as our military aid to the less developed world has declined, sales have increased, which means that there is less foreign exchange for other things. What is more serious, large quantities of arms which we gave or sold to our European allies are now becoming obsolete and are entering the international market. A surplus tank, for example, has a resale value about ten times its worth in scrap, and it is just as effective in putting down a rebellion as the most modern tank. This plus the fact that an increasing number of countries are becoming producers and entering the export market means that it will be more than ever difficult to exert restraint on the less developed countries.

The nations of the Third World bitterly resent outside efforts to limit their arms purchases; indeed, they hold that it is

* So many facts and statistics are cited in this section, it seems more convenient to write a bibliographical note. My principal sources are: a paper prepared by William B. Bader entitled "The Proliferation of Conventional Weapons" (to be published by Princeton University Press), which draws heavily on Congressional hearings and a staff study prepared by the Committee on Foreign Relations; "Dilemmas of the Arms Traffic," by Geoffrey Kemp (*Foreign Affairs,* January 1970), which draws on the work of Lincoln P. Bloomfield, John H. Hoagland and Amelia C. Leiss, his colleagues at M.I.T.; "The Arms Race and Defense Strategy in North Africa," a report of the American Universities Field Staff by Stuart H. Schaar, December 1967. Other sources are *The New York Times* and the *Department of State Bulletin.*

illegal under Article 51 of the United Nations Charter, which provides for the right of self-defense. Nevertheless, the United States has been the principal factor in such restraint as has been observed. Our leverage is modest, for where we have refused to sell sophisticated weapons in an effort to avoid a regional arms race, the Russians, the French and even the English have stepped in. Thus the Soviet Union moved to supply the Arab states when we refused Nasser the weapons he wanted for the war with Israel—introducing bombers and heavy tanks into the Middle East for the first time. When the United States announced that it would no longer sell weapons to South Africa, and the United Nations followed with a resolution calling on all members to do the same, France became the principal supplier, providing Mirage jets, helicopters, tanks, armored cars and coastal submarines. Similarly, our efforts to deter several Latin-American countries from buying sophisticated jets that were unneeded for legitimate defense have been sabotaged by Britain, France, Germany and Italy, all of whom have become arms suppliers to Latin America in the past three years. Brazil has now joined Peru in buying French supersonic fighter-bombers. From Britain, Argentina is acquiring Canberra jet bombers and two destroyers, while Brazil is buying two submarines. The civilian governments of Chile and Colombia are under enormous pressure to obtain similar weapons and will quite probably do so. As a result of all this, American resolve to refuse to sell sophisticated weapons in Latin America is weakening. If we agree to sell, we shall be accused of preferring profits to peace; if we refuse to sell, we shall be accused of seeking to dominate Latin America by keeping it weak.

In fact, military expenditures in Latin America have been grossly misrepresented. At least until very recently, defense budgets in Latin-American countries amounted to less than 2 percent of the hemisphere's combined GNP, compared to 4.5 percent in North Africa, 4.8 percent in Asia and 7.5 percent in the Middle East, where the Soviet Union and France are the principal suppliers. Moreover, 90 percent of these defense budgets in Latin America were for soft goods such as uniforms, barracks equipment, salaries and pensions; only 10 percent was devoted to arms. In 1968 Latin America's total annual outlays for military equipment were less than $200 million, "about half the annual cost of the New York Police Department." In terms of total governmental expenditures, Latin America was spending half as much for defense as it was in 1947. We should continue to bend every effort to restrain military spending in poor nations; but to insist that countries ought not to spend 12 percent of their over-all budgets for defense (the Latin-American average), while more than 57 percent of *our* federal expenditure was devoted to defense, could fairly be considered "arrogant," especially by a country such as Brazil, which is larger than the continental United States. Regrettably, military budgets in Latin America seem now to be on an upward curve, but the United States cannot be held responsible.

Finally, the notion that large military forces create political instability and the suppression of democratic institutions simply is not supported by the record. In Togo, a military coup and the assassination of the President was achieved by armed forces totaling three hundred men. Turkey has the largest military force in the Middle East and, except for Israel and Lebanon, is the only multiparty democracy. Indonesia's armed forces are much too large for so poor a country to bear, but it was not they who destroyed the fragile democratic institutions of that country. Venezuela invests heavily in military and police forces, and it is one of the most stable and democratic countries in Latin America.

The United States has been the largest supplier of arms in the postwar period primarily because for at least the first decade we were the only nation capable of exporting arms. Also, of some seventy new nations that emerged after 1945, all felt they must have defense forces and many sought them from the United States. For a time it was hoped that Africa might be

kept free of armaments in excess of what was absolutely necessary for maintaining internal order. But this proved illusory.
Except in Ethiopia, American arms sales in Africa have been
negligible, but France, which maintains military treaties with
twelve of its former African colonies, provides some $50 mil-
lion a year in military assistance to black Africa, exclusive of
the aid it provided to Biafra. In addition to its sales to South
Africa and to the illegal government of Rhodesia, France sells
weapons to Portugal for its war of attrition in Angola, Mozam-
bique and Guinea. (American weapons provided to Portugal
through NATO are at least theoretically prohibited from use
in Africa.) The total cynicism with which France operates in
the arms field is further demonstrated by its $400-million arms
deal with Libya, which includes heavy tanks and more than
one hundred Mirage fighter-bombers. In the early fifties, when
a devastated Western Europe seemed genuinely threatened
from the East, we granted France $4 billion in arms aid, by a
wide margin the largest amount for any country in the world.
It is ironic that France is now systematically undermining
American efforts on three continents to impose some moderation on existing or potential arms races and to avoid waste of
limited resources. In relation to its total industrial product,
France is probably the largest arms supplier in the world today.

Moreover, as a result of rearming the Arabs, the Soviet
Union has overtaken the United States in absolute terms. At
an ever-accelerating pace, the Russians have poured some $3
billion worth of armaments into the Middle East over the past
fourteen years. The bulk of it has gone to Egypt and Syria.
Less well known is the fact that Iraq has been supplied with
more MIG-21s than it had trained pilots to fly them; in numbers of sophisticated weapons generally it has been superior
to Iran, a country four times its size. When the Shah turned
to us for further arms, we refused, stalled and then offered to
sell a handful of advanced fighter-bombers for cash at a price
several times that at which Moscow sells its MIG-21s. Finally
in anger and frustration the Shah turned to the Soviet Union.

Stories of this kind can be multiplied many times, and in each case the country which finally feels obliged to turn to a new supplier thereby lowers its military efficiency through the diversity of its weapons, generally raises its operating costs and complicates its problems of obtaining and stocking spare parts.

In the year before the June 1967 war the Soviet Union shipped military equipment worth $200 million to Algeria—half of it as an outright gift. For what purpose did Algeria need 180 jet combat planes, four hundred tanks, and Styx missiles? Other than Israel some fifteen hundred miles to the east, its only natural enemy is Morocco. Though in population Morocco is the larger country, Algeria is believed to have a six- or seven-to-one advantage in military equipment, and its superiority over its other neighbor, Tunisia, is much greater. Understandably Morocco has pressed us hard for modern weapons, and again we stalled—not to avoid an arms race, for Algeria is already out of sight, but because we wanted to see Morocco's resources invested more productively. Soviet military aid to Algeria has been so far beyond any conceivable need that it seems quite apparent that Algeria is being used as a supply base from which Soviet arms can be more conveniently shipped to other points in Africa and the Middle East when occasion arises.

Another indication of our tough attitude toward providing arms was our refusal to assist Nigeria in putting down the Biafran rebellion. Not only did we decline to give military assistance, but we refused to license exports through private channels for payment in cash. The result was that the Soviet Union became (with Britain) the chief arms supplier of a nation that had had no prior dealings with the Communist world. Meanwhile, as we have seen, France prolonged a particularly cruel and senseless war by arming Biafra. In neither case was a vital national interest involved: Russia sought influence; France hoped for oil and the breakup of the largest nation in Africa.

Nor will critics of American arms policies find a parallel to the Soviet arming of Indonesia, a country without threatening enemies. Cynically catering to the vanity of Sukarno, the Russians pumped more than $1 billion in armaments into what was then probably the most fiscally irresponsible nation in the world. It should be no surprise to the Russians that this sum is still owed them, as part of Indonesia's $2.2 billion of external debt.

On the understandable but simplistic assumption that peddling arms *must* be bad, a legion of critics from Senator Eugene McCarthy to the far fringes of the left have asserted that the United States has been wholly irresponsible in its program of military aid and sales. The record shows, on the contrary, that we have been fairly restrained, at least in the less developed world. We have made an effort to see that arms were suited to the real security needs of the nations involved. The vast majority of weapons we provided were for nations under attack or nations which with reason felt under genuine threat of attack. And, almost without exception, they were given to the weak to counterbalance the power of a stronger neighbor. We have not defied world opinion, except, as in Vietnam, where our own forces became mortally involved. We have turned down many more requests than we have filled; indeed, on every occasion when the U. N. General Assembly has voted overwhelmingly for arms limitations, more than half of those voting in favor were even then applying to the United States for arms.

The United States has recognized this problem of proliferating arms sales for a considerable time, even though no solution has been found. In recent years, Congress has placed a ceiling (currently $385 million annually) on arms that can be sold on credit. Speaking to the Eighteen-Nation Disarmament Conference in 1966, the President of the United States said:

> As we focus on nuclear arms, let us not forget that resources are being devoted to nonnuclear arms races all around the world. These resources might be better spent on feeding the hungry, healing the sick and teaching the uneducated.

The cost of acquiring and maintaining one squadron of supersonic aircraft diverts resources that would build and maintain a university. We suggest therefore that countries, on a regional basis, explore ways to limit competition among themselves for costly weapons often sought for reasons of illusory prestige.

So far, there has not been the slightest response. Nor has there been any concerted effort by the United Nations or any other international body to damp down the bull market in conventional weapons. Two fairly innocuous U. N. resolutions proposing public registry of all grants and sales of military equipment—one introduced in 1965, the second in 1968—failed to arouse interest, much less a majority. The American President made a similar proposal with respect to the Middle East, but it was neither taken up nor followed up.

Most observers are pessimistic as to what can be accomplished to curb the growth of conventional weapons. They point out that an apparently insatiable demand is matched by an increasing number of producers for whom foreign sales are not only profitable but essential for economic production. As the advanced nations convert to more modern weapons, the quantities of surplus equipment is constantly growing. The end of the war in Vietnam, it is feared, will result in millions of dollars' worth of arms entering the international market. The pessimists also point out that efforts to cut off or limit arms sales may simply lead to greater self-sufficiency in arms through local manufacture, as in the case of South Africa, Argentina and Israel. Under French license, Argentina is manufacturing tanks which it hopes to sell throughout the hemisphere. Finally, if the United States withdraws a significant proportion of its forces from Europe and Asia and at the same time restricts arms sales, panic may be created in many capitals.

Others contend that since no serious effort has been made to cope with these problems, we cannot know whether there are feasible solutions. William Bader, who was a staff consultant to the Senate Foreign Relations Committee, points out that virtually nothing has been done in this field; even serious research is confined largely to two institutions, one at M.I.T. and the other in Stockholm. He believes that the proposal for reporting arms sales can win majority support in the General Assembly if it is presented "not as an arms control measure . . . but as a straightforward effort to provide the Secretary General with statistics on arms transfers as a means of lifting some of the regional distress and anxieties . . ." He further suggests that, until confidence can be established, reporting be confined to major pieces of military equipment such as tanks, aircraft and armed personnel carriers, which are difficult to hide. If successful, a measure of this kind would provide a better understanding of the dimensions of the problem and focus attention on the serious trouble spots.

More problematical is whether regional groups such as the Organization of African Unity and the Organization of American States could negotiate agreements prohibiting specified kinds of sophisticated (and expensive) weapons, such as missiles, supersonic aircraft and heavy tanks. Since the serious security problems of Latin-American and African countries are all internal, such weapons simply are not needed.

Much more within our own power to act is the suggestion that arms-sales agreements include provisions requiring that at the end of its useful life major equipment be either scrapped or returned to the original seller at a predetermined price. Although in fact we have the right of veto over the resale of arms that we have provided (with a very few exceptions), in the event this right has proven difficult to exercise. More important, we have no control over the disposition of arms after the first resale. For example, some years ago the Federal Republic of Germany obtained U. S. approval for the sale of one hundred obsolete fighter planes to Iran, which promptly resold them to Pakistan against our wishes. We ought to have the power to prevent such transactions. One way to do so would be to have fixed agreements that all major types of U. S. arms, by whatever means acquired, would be returned or scrapped for a fixed price (Bader suggests 7.5 percent of the original price), which would be applied as a credit against future sales.

The reason for examining this problem in some detail is that it is a seriously neglected and misunderstood subject to which more attention ought to be given. One wishes that the intellectual energy and moral fervor now devoted to damning the United States out of hand could be focused constructively on such real dilemmas as this, where more imaginative solutions and a lot of political determination are required if we are to fulfill our obligations responsibly.

CONDUCTING FOREIGN POLICY IN A DEMOCRACY

No one ever claimed that democracy was an easy way of conducting the nation's business. It is hard enough under a parliamentary system, where there is no separation of powers between the executive and the legislature, and where political parties exert some discipline on their members. Under the American Constitution the executive and the legislature are in an adversary relationship, and in the area of foreign relations their respective powers and responsibilities are by no means clear. The President has the authority to conduct the nation's foreign policy, and as Commander in Chief of the armed forces he clearly has primary responsibility for defense and the conduct of wars. On the other hand, Congress not only must provide the funds necessary to make policies effective, but specifically has the authority for raising armies and for declaring war, while treaties must be approved by the Senate.

At various times in our history the executive or the Congress has so forcefully asserted its powers that the demise of the other branch was regularly forecast. The system of checks and balances written into the Constitution was believed to be failing. The imbalance was probably never so real as it appeared, yet as recently as the 1920s, after Congress had demolished President Wilson's foreign policy, and a succession of weak Presidents followed, it was said that the executive would never again assert itself over the will of Congress. With Franklin D. Roosevelt the tables were turned once again, and since then—largely as a result of circumstance—the executive has been considered dominant.

Now we are in a period when Congress is again striving to assert itself. The executive is being accused of usurping the powers of Congress through the indiscriminate use of executive orders, and Congress is being accused—often by its own members—of defaulting on its responsibilities. Congressmen speak of a constitutional crisis. They remind the President and the public that only Congress has the authority to declare war, although in fact it has never done so, but has merely formalized a state of hostilities already existing. In 1970 it sought to rescind four important joint resolutions—such as that of the Tonkin Gulf—which had, depending on one's interpretation of the Constitution, either granted powers to the President or merely confirmed and approved those he already had.

Understandably, most criticism of American foreign policy and execution focuses on the executive branch, but historians looking back on this period may well find more serious dereliction of duty on the part of Congress, which has been unconstructive, unimaginative and stultified by its leadership. If the new self-criticism among its members leads merely to a more concerted effort to limit the powers of the executive, little will have been accomplished and it is conceivable that much harm will be done. What is needed is genuine reform of Congress.

In an age of change, only Congress remains immovable, complaining of its loss of powers, but unwilling to make those minimum reforms which might endow it with greater respect and make it more effective and responsive. Perhaps the oldest and most serious complaint against Congress is the seniority system, or government by the survival of the least fit. It is not merely a matter of the age of committee chairmen, though thirteen are over seventy years old, six are over seventy-five, and two are over eighty. What is more appalling is the power they wield and the abject manner in which the full membership bends to their will. The committee system

> cuts loose the most powerful men in Congress from the control of the parties and tends to put the parties in their control. And it gives this power to men few of whom speak for broadly representative constituencies. They are the men who come, by and large, from the safe states and districts, from the economic and cultural islands of the country. This system by which Congress organizes itself into satrapies is probably the largest single reason for the unresponsiveness of the legislature and the disjointedness of our government. Yet nothing in our Constitution requires Congress to be organized as it is.*

If reformers want a worthy target for their energies, here is one. Committee chairmen should be chosen by party caucus, and their term should be limited to four consecutive years.

Except for ending secrecy in voting, the reforms voted by Congress in the autumn of 1970 were utterly inconsequential. Efforts to end the seniority system were defeated by 2 to 1 in the Senate. Although Congress already has some three hundred committees and subcommittees, which ensures that no serious problem can be looked at whole, one of the "reforms" consisted of adding another standing committee in the Senate. Nothing was done to speed up the legislative process; to end the absurdity of annual authorization for continuing programs; to prohibit committee meetings while sessions of the House or Senate are in progress; to stop the inexcusable practice of attaching riders to bills as a means of pushing through controversial legislation on the coattails of popular measures; or to provide members with more adequate resources for research and information. In short, nothing was done to make the Congress more efficient, responsive and responsible.

One of the most insidious aspects of the seniority system is

* Charles Frankel, *High on Foggy Bottom* (New York: Harper & Row, 1969), p. 235.

its effect on the executive branch. If all committee chairmen were philosopher kings, the relationship between Congress and the executive would still be a difficult one, with each side jealous of its prerogatives and inclined to feel that it best represented the public good. As it is, what the Constitution has made an adversary situation, circumstances have made actively hostile in many instances. Because committee chairmen are often unrepresentative and use their powers unpredictably and arbitrarily, they are too frequently looked upon by Administration officials with fear or scorn and are treated as fools to be duped or cajoled. Committee chairmen respond with distrust and that arrogance with which elective office appears to endow legislators in the presence of mere appointed officials. Thus Congressmen have treated some of our most eminent public servants as flunkies to be browbeaten in public hearings or pawns in their private game of politics with the President. Too often they are shown respect only if they say what the committee chairman wants to hear.

This situation is aggravated by the fact that many bills must go through eight committees, with hearings in each that consume an inordinate amount of time. High government officials must be present on demand, but there is no penalty for Congressional absenteeism. Only on rare and newsworthy occasions is a majority present. Too frequently those Congressmen who can best afford the time for committee hearings are those intellectually ossified members in safe seats who need to devote little energy to staying in office. Many Congressmen, including some of the most competent, admit they spend as much as 60 percent of their working day doing favors for their constituents or otherwise trying to insure that they will win the next election. This leaves little time or energy for the increasingly heavy work load or for developing that degree of expertise in at least half a dozen subjects that will make them really useful and competent legislators.

That members of the House must seek reelection every two years is regrettable, for it does not give them the freedom that

Senators enjoy to attend to important business. Being required by the Constitution, the two-year term cannot be easily changed, although the effort should be made. But many of the ills of Congress could be altered merely by changing rules and procedures adopted by Congress itself. The present organization of committees is not decreed by law, nor is there a requirement that money bills go through the Congressional mill twice—first authorization, then appropriation—thereby adding thousands of man hours to the burdens of both the legislative and executive branches. It certainly ensures neither careful nor reasoned consideration. Congressional appropriations have often been increased or decreased by 20 percent or more without any substantive discussion of the program or agency involved, but on the whim or grudge of a committee chairman, or a Congressional mood that is unrelated to the issue in hand.

Members of Congress complain bitterly about executive secrecy, asserting that on grounds of security information is withheld from them that they rightly should know. There are grounds for this charge and it could be debated at length: right to know versus need to know; whether in fact much information is overclassified; whether information is withheld for political rather than security reasons. Clearly members of Congress ought to have information not available to the general public, but the sorry fact is that the executive branch simply does not trust many members of Congress, and with some reason. It is hard enough to maintain discipline within the executive branch, where the inspired leak has become a way of life, but the President has no control whatever over members of Congress who may be antagonistic to him and not above using privileged information for political purposes. And when lawmakers are granted a confidence, it may be assumed that word will spread at least as far as their staffs.

The danger of giving away military secrets is perhaps less troublesome than betraying political intentions which may be of great use to potential enemies. For example, in March 1970 the Secretary of State assured the Senate Foreign Relations

Committee in closed session that the Administration had no plans to send ground troops into Laos. In less than a fortnight, the chairman of that committee had betrayed this confidence, thereby signaling to the North Vietnamese, possibly erroneously, that as far as the United States was concerned they had a free hand in Laos.

No nation in the world conducts so much delicate and dangerous business in such a glare of publicity. The whole world is not only watching what we do but listening to what we say to one another publicly—and even privately. It is a hard way to make policy, or to carry it out. As a people we believe profoundly in the public's right to know, to the point where we rather congratulate ourselves when our press publishes a confidential memorandum from a government official to the President. In going so far, we compound the natural advantage of totalitarian states, which do not have to talk in public. They do not have to explain, justify or wheedle. They cannot wholly ignore public opinion, but they can do their political infighting in private. They do not have legislators whose objective is to embarrass the government, who ask impossible questions and threaten retribution if they do not get answers, who ask to be taken into the confidence of the executive and then betray those confidences. And what the legislators don't put under the spotlight, the press will.

A friendly observer of the Senate has noted that the question to be asked is not what role do Senators play in foreign-policy-making, but what role does foreign-policy-making play in the lives of Senators. "Most senators enter foreign policy for what it can do for them back home. . . . Senators cover foreign policy as firemen cover fires; they rush to the scene only when the building is in flames."*

We shall see in a later chapter some of the more specific ways in which Congress has failed to fulfill its function in matters of national security as a result of its antiquated organiza-

* Hugh Gregory Gallagher, *Advise and Obstruct: The Role of the U. S. Senate in Foreign Policy Decisions* (New York: Delacorte, 1969), pp. 31-32.

tion and ineffectual procedures. What needs to be pointed out here is the way in which these shortcomings aggravate one of the most serious dangers inherent in conducting foreign policy in a democracy. This is the temptation in the executive branch to oversell particular programs and policies. The adversary relationship between the executive and Congress plus the need for public support almost assures that the Administration will overstate its case in order to obtain passage of necessary legislation. Out of this dilemma arises much of the grounds for criticism which have been discussed in earlier chapters. It helps, too, to explain why honest men often appear dishonest and why "the credibility gap" is often believed to be a euphemism for lying.

More than half the time in these postwar years, the President's party has been a minority in both houses of Congress. This has been less important than it might seem, for, as there is no party discipline, majorities must be built of fluctuating elements in both parties. Almost every issue requires a new majority, which must be created with the help of willful committee chairmen, or in spite of them if necessary.

Under these circumstances members of the executive branch justify to themselves playing on the soft spots of committee chairmen, restricting candor and manipulating public opinion to bring pressure on Congress. Thus, for example, Presidents, Secretaries of State and lesser officials have appealed for what they deemed necessary in the language of anti-Communism which they only half believed. This has been particularly marked in the case of foreign aid and is one reason it is now in trouble.

There was a very strong case in 1947 for our assuming responsibilities in Greece which Britain could no longer afford. But the language in which the Truman Doctrine was presented to Congress appealed more heavily to emotions than was desirable, and it was broader in scope than was necessary. Ambassador Bohlen relates that General Marshall (then on his way to Moscow) first saw the text in Paris and cabled the

President questioning the wisdom of stressing anti-Communism so heavily and suggesting that he was "overstating the case a bit." Truman replied that from all his contacts with the Senate it was clear to him that this was the only way the measure could be passed.*

It is easy to dismiss this as simple dishonesty, but where men who bear the burdens of responsibility believe deeply in the necessity of some action, especially where national security is thought to be involved, they would be more than human if they did not present it in its most palatable form. What is perhaps more serious is that they begin to believe their own effusions as a precise definition of reality. This is not to say that the dangers our leaders saw in the late forties and since have been imagined; rather, the language in which they have been discussed has been inflated, with the result that we have appeared more of everything than we were—more anti-Communist, more aggressive, more fearful. Meanwhile the general frustration of the public has been aggravated by its incapacity to distinguish between the merits of a particular measure and the language in which it was couched.

Institutional reform will not alter the adversary relationship which is built into our constitutional system of checks and balances. But if committee chairmen attained their posts on the basis of respect of their peers in each house instead of longevity and the accident of geography, if their powers were limited and their sense of responsibility to *all* the people expanded, it would be far more difficult for the executive branch to assume that the ends justified the means. Mutual respect between the two branches of government—now gravely lacking—would be possible, and this would be the beginning of more responsible government.

The dilemma of conducting foreign policy in a democracy will remain. How much candor can a democratic government afford? How much *must* it afford? Clearly, more than we have

* Charles E. Bohlen, *The Transformation of American Foreign Policy* (New York: W. W. Norton, 1969), p. 87.

had. But no one expects Moscow to announce in advance its strategy for conducting the arms limitation talks, much less what strategic weapons it has or is planning and why. No one expects the Hanoi government to advise its people of its strategy—or whether it has one—in the Paris negotiations. But comparable information seems expected of Washington, and less than full candor is interpreted as a willful effort to mislead the American people (which may be the case) rather than an effort to leave the enemy or antagonist in some small state of uncertainty (which is more probable). Propaganda has been defined as "that branch of the art of lying which consists of very nearly deceiving your friends without quite deceiving your enemies."* This is a danger wherever candor is qualified.

What the public is entitled to know—indeed, must know to exercise its responsibilities—will always be a matter of debate. The answer will depend on one's analysis of the dangers to which the republic is exposed and one's confidence in its leaders. It is not surprising that those who are disposed to assume that the dangers are imagined are most inclined to believe that our leaders are untrustworthy. But they will not find a revolutionary society where the public is so well or fully informed, or where the public has a greater opportunity to influence policy. Hence critics would do well to work toward those reforms, especially in Congress, which will make the conduct of foreign policy in a democracy more effective.

* F. M. Cornford, *Microcosmographia Academica* (Cambridge: Bowes & Bowes), preface to the 1922 edition.

X

Institutions
of Power

POWER, AS a concept and as an instrument, has become such an obsession today that it may be useful to examine some of the institutions affecting American foreign policy which are endowed—or thought to be endowed—with that quicksilver quality.

A recent immigrant from Eastern Europe has observed that whereas the American intellectual rebel yearns for power,

> the Eastern European rebelling intellectual does not miss power. He knows only too well the leaden burden it is. Instead, all he dreams about is influence. He realizes that in enlarging the margins of freedom and human dignity, influence is more useful than power. The less visible he remains, the better his chances for gaining influence in a totalitarian society. What he dreams is what his American counterpart rejects with disgust.*

This is worth pondering. Most people who have held power are less impressed by it than those who have not. They better understand how frequently power is a negative force (to obstruct, to destroy) and how much skill and imagination is

* Leopold Tyrmand, "Revolutionaries: European vs. American," *The New York Times Magazine*, Feb. 15, 1970, p. 25.

177

required to turn it to constructive purposes. This is the American dilemma. The ultimate in the negativism of power is symbolized by the atomic bomb, whose only function is to prevent its use by others.

But we are speaking here of political power, which in this country is so diffuse that no one holds very much of it; even Presidents, who hold the largest piece, are aware how conditional their power is. A ukase issued by the White House can be extraordinarily ineffective if it does not have considerable support among those who must carry it out. Even a President's commands do not need to be disobeyed to have their purpose defeated. They can be observed in the letter and not the spirit; they can be talked to death, put in a bottom drawer, willfully misunderstood or followed with such indiscriminate zeal as to make them ridiculous. The President too must use influence, must lead. For others, whose orders do not carry the force of law, the difficulties of wielding power are even more tricky, and this is one reason good executives are paid high salaries.

"Black Influence" may not be an effective rallying cry, but it is probably a more accurate description of what blacks want, and have the capacity to get, than "Black Power." Similarly with other groups, organizations and institutions. We have seen the power of small groups to incapacitate the nation, but it is not easy to translate this negative power into positive influence, say, to obtain higher wages. What disaffected groups want or ought to want, what they envy in others, is really influence. The powers of a great bank or a major corporation are highly circumscribed—by laws, by custom, by competitors, by clients, by its position in the limelight—but its influence is substantial. To many this will seem an irrelevant or spurious distinction, but it is important to an understanding of how things happen and of the relative success of American democracy.

THE ESTABLISHMENT

One of the many beliefs shared by left and right in America is that an all-powerful and generally malevolent Establishment, a conspiratorial alliance of bankers, businessmen, foundation executives and a few chosen intellectuals, exerts an unwarranted and largely uncontrollable influence on government. In the opinion of the right, the Establishment is a "secret government" unaccountable to the public and composed of "do-gooders" and fellow travelers who are leading the United States into bankruptcy, socialism and world government. Seen from the left, the Establishment is a power structure unresponsive to the public and composed of impervious men who care only to promote their own financial interests, even if it means intervention and war.

The term "Establishment" was first used in the United Kingdom at a time when the British were coming to realize that their democracy was flawed by lingering class consciousness and social rigidity. If the aristocracy was losing its wealth through high taxation, it was nevertheless clinging to its power by rewarding its own. Too frequently, birth and breeding were still requirements for attaining positions of influence and prestige. What was seen as a closed fraternity of those who were of the nobility or who had attended the right schools and one of the two great universities became known as "the Establishment."

However, the term was quickly imported to the United States and is now in common parlance worldwide, though without the same degree of definition. So useful a term for identifying the undefinable could not be resisted. It is now all things to all men—a convenient label for that mysterious "they" who seem to affect our lives and who from time immemorial have been envied, feared, hated, resented and admired because, though unidentified, they appeared to have the attributes of power. Or it may be used so broadly as to include everyone who has any influence or position and who appears opposed to change. The meaning used here is more limited.

In America, the Establishment concept had much to feed on: the conspiracy theory which Communism caused to be popularized and which became a fever with President Kennedy's assassination; the historical resentment of the West toward the sources of wealth in the East; the tensions between North and South that have existed since the Civil War. If the United States had no aristocracy, there were class distinctions waiting to be made on both sides between those who had attended the older private institutions of the East and those who had attended the state-supported universities which predominated elsewhere, between WASPs and others, between those who came from Europe earlier and those who came later. And of course there were racial distinctions.

Yet it is demonstrable that no country in the world lends itself so poorly to the Establishment concept as the United States. Not only are sources of power here more diversified, but geographically they are scattered as nowhere else and becoming more so all the time. In the less developed nations there is inevitably an Establishment of sorts composed of that small minority which has education and position. No one can doubt that the Communist countries have Establishments, for there power is closely held. In London, Paris, Rome, the men of power and influence see each other every day, lunch at the same clubs, go to the same parties. In most countries, government, law, banking, business, communications, the arts, all focus on one city. In the United States there is no such focus of interests or influence. The most powerful men in Congress are not even on the fringes of the Establishment, as most come from rural areas of the South and Southwest. Even the Cabinet is short on Establishment figures.

Nevertheless, let us examine what little substance there is to the notion that a group of nonofficial persons on the northeastern seaboard has a controlling or exorbitant influence on the foreign policy of the United States. Since critics of the Establishment have in some cases named names of individuals and organizations considered representative of the Establishment, one can have reasonable confidence that he is looking at the phenomenon referred to.

Doubtless a member of the New Left or the John Birch Society would find in the group a certain homogeneity, for the spectrum of opinion represented has limits which are unacceptable to either one. To almost anyone else, the range would seem wide indeed—inevitably so, composed as the group is of scholars and men of affairs, of bankers and civil servants, of labor leaders and Congressmen, of young men and old. About all that they may be said to have in common is an interest in international affairs, a belief that the United States has a role to play in those affairs, and a bias in favor of orderly change. Some believe that the United States (Vietnam aside) is overcommitted abroad; others feel that extensive involvement is inevitable or salutary or both. Some believe that private enterprise not only is good at home but is the only way that the Third World will lift itself out of poverty; others believe that a large element of socialism is necessary and are often highly critical of American business abroad. Almost all believe in international cooperation; virtually none believes world government is feasible, but many would consider it a desirable, if distant, objective.

Moreover, this so-called foreign-policy Establishment has a generation gap within it that, if less sharp, is no less marked than in other groups. The younger men tend, for example, to place less confidence in NATO, to be more flexible in their approaches to the Soviet Union and China, to put less weight on the potential influence of the United States and to be more willing to run risks to achieve arms limitations.

The notion of an Establishment as a tight little island of like-thinking opinion-makers is, then, far from the mark. To the extent that a foreign-policy Establishment exists, it is both mobile and fluid. "Membership" is based primarily on the individual's capacity to influence the thinking of others, which in turn is an amalgam of that individual's intellectual powers as judged by his peers and his experience in positions of responsibility. There is a constant influx of new members and a departure of others, either because of age or because their attention is diverted into other fields or because, for a variety of reasons, they are no longer listened to.

Whether there is in fact a foreign-policy Establishment in any consequential sense and, if so, what it truly consists of is unhappily less important than what outsiders think it is. The reason for discussing so nebulous a subject at all is to disabuse those who believe that foreign-policy decisions are being made outside the normal and responsible channels of government, or that those decisions are being affected by an influential minority in a manner inimical to American interests. In truth, the alleged Establishment contains a range of moderate opinion that is highly representative of the United States as a whole. If it is "internationalist"—whatever that term means—it is a less pronounced bias than that of businessmen who believe in business or labor leaders who believe in labor unions or doctors who believe in medicine.

If one doubts the assertion that there is no consensus within the Establishment, if one believes it is capable of reaching collective decisions, one must explain how it imposes these decisions or otherwise exerts power, for it has no lobby and no organization for reaching decisions, much less imposing them on government. If there is one issue on which it might be possible to obtain something like a consensus, it would be the need for more foreign aid—a field in which the United States is doing less and less.

What we do undoubtedly have on the northeastern seaboard, as one would expect, is a heavy concentration of knowledge of and experience in international affairs. It consists of serious students who have thought deeply on issues of American foreign policy whether as academics, investment bankers, public servants or whatever. Despite the enormous range of opinion they represent on specific issues, they understandably share certain premises and, undoubtedly, biases: they do not favor promoting revolution and they do not wish to see a return to isolationism. Such influence as they have is exerted as individuals, not as a group. No doubt John J. McCloy and John Kenneth Galbraith have contacts in Washington that can hardly be equaled, but they are giving radically different advice to those who are making decisions, and both are considered preeminent members of the Establishment. Only those who are not in it believe that it exists as a cohesive power in foreign policy.

Rather than being a menace or a deterrent to change, the foreign-policy Establishment has developed most of the fresh ideas and concepts that have evolved in the field. For example, it was the Establishment rather than the military that first gained a comprehension of the implications of nuclear weapons and developed strategies for coping with them. It was in the Establishment that new concepts took shape to solve serious international financial problems. It has provided a pool of informed generalists and experts who could be called to service in the executive branch. Perhaps, most important, it has been a source of continuity in the conduct of foreign policy, preventing radical swings to right or left.

Nevertheless, it must be acknowledged that the Establishment bears a heavy responsibility for the tardiness with which its members spoke out openly against Vietnam. Here they did not lead but followed. For the most part they did not favor U. S. policies in Southeast Asia, but until too late felt constrained to remain silent, on the grounds that there was no honorable way out and that outright opposition would only give comfort to Hanoi. They were more conscious than most that Ho Chi Minh had beaten the French in Paris, not Vietnam, and that Ho's strategy against the United States was the same. Sensitive to the consequences of unilateral withdrawal and aggrieved by the oversimplifications of the extreme critics, they were perhaps too prone to intellectualize a problem which no longer had a satisfactory resolution. We will never know whether, if American opinion had held firm in support of the government, our minimum objectives might have been reached with less killing rather than more; the idea cannot be dismissed out of hand. However this may be, when it became evident that our objectives could no longer justify the means for attaining them, the Establishment should have exerted greater influence sooner in an effort to achieve a reversal of policy.

Historically, nations have been in the deepest trouble when their Establishments lost confidence in themselves—and this is the case today in the United States. This was true in France before and after World War II; it was true in Britain in the sixties; it was true in the United States at the time of the surrender to Joseph McCarthy; and it is again true today, when a sense of defensiveness about Vietnam has undermined not merely confidence but values which do not deserve to be cast away.

THE MILITARY-INDUSTRIAL COMPLEX

One of the few observations of President Eisenhower that is quoted favorably by non-Republicans is his warning about the military-industrial complex. This concern extends through a very wide spectrum of the population, as it properly should. Even if the motives and judgments of its members were wholly benign, one would have reason to worry about a set of institutions which consumes 8 percent of our gross national product, which has until very recently absorbed more than half the federal budget and on which millions of Americans depend for their livelihood. More than half of the gross national product of the state of Washington derives from the federal goverment. The Pentagon is by far the largest organization in the world; when to this is added all the defense-related industries, their employees and dependents, all the retired officers and veterans organizations, one must reckon with a formidable force in American society, even though it would be a mistake to suppose that all its members think alike or are conscious of being part of a potent pressure group.

Adam Yarmolinsky, who has edited and co-authored the

definitive work* on the impact of the military on American society, points out that even if the defense budget were reduced by ten to twenty billion dollars, as it may be, it will still be incomparably the largest element in our government operations and will therefore remain a matter of concern. He also testifies, on the basis of his own experience in the Pentagon, that in none of the most controversial decisions involving the use of American forces abroad did the uniformed military play a controlling part. In the Bay of Pigs episode, theirs was not the dominating role; in the Cuban missile crisis, they were overruled by the President; in the Dominican Republic affair they were hardly consulted; and in Vietnam they urged neither our initial involvement nor the later massive intervention nor the bombing of the North. Once we were in, to be sure, they pressed for larger forces and greater freedom of action; and once bombing of the North had started, they opposed and effectively delayed suspending it. There is a sharp difference of opinion as to whether they were instrumental in persuading the President to invade Cambodia, but if they were, they can hardly be faulted. In battle it is their job to seize military opportunity; it is for others to weigh the political and human consequences. Nor was this an issue on which the weight of the military-industrial complex was brought to bear. Its influence is more generalized, more subtle—and therefore more difficult to deal with. Doubtless, however, it shaped the environment in which the President's decision was made.

Thus, the danger of the military-industrial complex is real enough, but it need not be portrayed as a conspiratorial alliance between the uniformed military and industrial barons. Generals and admirals always want more of everything; to be prepared for every contingency is their responsibility. But they do not make policy, they do not aspire to make policy and they cannot be blamed for mistakes of policy. To blame them

* *The Military Establishment: An Examination of Its Impact on American Society,* a study sponsored by the Twentieth Century Fund, published by Harper & Row.

for their many errors of judgment within their own area of responsibility is enough. Obviously they influence policy, as do many other groups in our society, but it is still made by civilians, who, by the standards of an earlier day, impose many burdensome restraints upon them. This is not to deny that the military have much to account for, but usurping the authority of our elected leaders is not one of them. And if we are to restrain the power of the military-industrial complex, we shall have to look to ourselves and our civilian leaders.

Until very recently Congress insisted on appropriating more funds for defense than the executive branch asked for and had been agreed upon by the military. Indeed, high-ranking civilians in the Pentagon (at least under McNamara) say that, in their efforts to achieve moderation, efficiency and economy in the military establishment, their problem is not with the generals or the admirals or the representatives of industry, to whom they can stand up, but with members of Congress, to whom they cannot. This is not to say that the military-industrial complex does not exert influence on members of Congress —only that members of Congress, and especially the chairmen of the key committees, have been a more receptive audience than officials of the executive branch. It would be interesting to know how some of the key chairmen in both houses, who in the early fifties believed that a defense budget of more than $13 billion would lead to national bankruptcy, found it possible to press throughout the sixties for ever larger military budgets till they had passed $70 billion. It was the pressure of Congress more than anything else which precluded, until recently, the shedding of the illusion that nuclear superiority over the Soviets was either necessary or relevant. And almost certainly it was pressure from Congress which finally induced the President, against Mr. McNamara's better judgment, to deploy anti-ballistic missiles (ABM).

Though the tide has now turned in Congress, and defense proposals are being more critically scrutinized, the ABM story reflects little credit on our legislators—either pro or con

—if one goes back of 1969. Ten years earlier, the Army had wanted to deploy a primitive ABM system, the Nike-Zeus, at a cost of $13–14 billion. This and subsequent efforts were resisted by three Administrations, although the issue remained active, and research and development continued. In 1966 Congress appropriated $168 million "to prepare" for production of the Nike-X. The following year the Senate Appropriations Committee went on record as favoring deployment of Nike-X, and the Administration, while still deferring a decision, felt obliged to ask Congress for $377 million—again for preparation, in case "talks with the Soviet Union fail." At that time Russia had not even agreed to talks, and the possibility of achieving agreement on arms limitations within the next fiscal year was, to say the least, improbable.

Then, in September 1967, in a painful exercise in doubletalk, Mr. McNamara announced the Administration's decision to begin deployment of a thin ABM system estimated to cost $5 billion. The reaction from abroad and in the American press was highly unfavorable, but in general the decision created less stir than the announcement of McNamara's resignation two months later.

What is at issue here is not whether the decision to deploy Sentinel was right or wrong, but that Congress did not even appear to understand what was involved—that this was the most critical decision in many years and might have profound consequences. Despite a mounting tide of serious articles and informed letters to the editor analyzing the issues involved, Congress manifested virtually no concern. Seven months elapsed before the Senate Preparedness Subcommittee called hearings, and then they were quite perfunctory. Not until May did Congressional opposition begin to organize. After a minimum of floor debate, efforts to defeat the measure failed in July; a second effort in October failed by an even wider margin.

The next year—1969—the story was altogether different. For reasons which cannot altogether be explained by the change in Administration, Congress suddenly became aroused. ABM became *the* issue, and a band of Congressmen set out to defeat it—with or without really understanding the issues. The results were almost as depressing as the year before. After virtually no debate in 1968, there was a surfeit in 1969; it became emotional, unserious and uninstructive. Moreover, what was possible in 1968 proved impossible in 1969: the proponents of deployment became more entrenched, interests and positions became fixed. And, above all, an Administration which did not really believe in ballistic-missile defense, one which had given Congress what it believed was wanted in anticipation of a Presidential election, was replaced by an Administration more thoroughly convinced of the need for ABM. What was particularly irritating was the mantle of virtue which the Congressional opponents cast over themselves as they went into the battle which should have been fought at least a year earlier.

The story was much the same with respect to MIRV—multiple independently targeted reentry vehicle—which has the potential for seriously undermining the basis of nuclear deterrence. Members of Congress now say they knew nothing about it, that the Pentagon kept it a secret even from them. Perhaps so, but *The New York Times* gave a full and fairly accurate description of MIRV in the early autumn of 1967,* and informed people—which one presumes includes members of Congress—knew of its existence much earlier. Yet not until 1969 could one detect any Congressional concern about the consequences of the continued testing and approaching deployment of MIRV. As with ABM, conditions were by then much less propitious for delaying its development.

In the spring of 1969 a group of liberal members of Congress—those on whom sensible control of the military-industrial complex will heavily depend—sat down with a number of intellectuals to confer for two days on how, in the words of

* In a signed column by Robert Kleiman, Oct. 9, 1967.

one of their number, they could "dismantle the national security state." The report subsequently published by the Congressional sponsors is not encouraging, for it suggests that the problem is quite simply one of taking an axe to our defense forces. Take, for example, this remarkable and unchallenged statement: "Few world situations are imaginable in which this country would not have adequate time to build from its large reserves and enormous productive capacity should danger arise."* This, of course, is the premise on which this country operated for 170 years, but it is astounding to see its resurrection today when the United States is vulnerable every minute of every day, when West Berlin could be captured in an hour and Western Europe overrun in forty-eight, if there were no adequate countervailing forces. The strategic assumption of the past twenty years has been that if the need arose we would have to fight with forces in being, and since the early sixties it has been argued persuasively that if deterrence is to be credible, we need to have a variety of forces capable of responding to aggression at the lowest level of violence consistent with effective defense. If we have no means to resist a probing action in Berlin, where our will has repeatedly been tested, or to deal with a less than all-out attack on Western Europe, our nuclear deterrent becomes meaningless for the defense of Europe; for no one believes that we will use nuclear weapons in an ambiguous situation.

Or again, one of the participants could assert, without rebuttal, that a military budget of between 10 and 25 percent of present levels "would be more than sufficient." This, of course, would mean unilateral disarmament on a vast scale; it would mean the abandonment of Europe, as well as many other obligations we have undertaken, and a retreat into a very shaky Fortress America. The American people are simply not prepared to expose themselves and their allies to the mercies of self-proclaimed enemies, however frequently we are reassured

---

* *American Militarism 1970*, edited by Erwin Knoll and Judith Nies McFadden (New York: Viking, 1969), p. 38.

about their good intentions. If we are to get the American military budget under better control—as we must—more constructive suggestions than this will have to be made.

It is often forgotten that Secretary of State Dulles' much ridiculed threat of massive retaliation arose precisely because at that time the West lacked forces to defend itself by other means. When the United States itself was still invulnerable, the threat was believable, however objectionable it sounded. Today, those who advocate cutting the military budget to 10 or 25 percent of present levels cannot offer even this alternative, for the threat of massive retaliation would mean nothing or it would mean mass suicide.

Another conference proposal for dealing with the military budget was that Congress "should begin by holding budget hearings in Congressional districts and in the states, asking the American people how they want their money spent, whether they want to continue spending the largest portion of their tax dollar on the Vietnam war and future wars."* Thus might Congress substitute one outrageous default of responsibility for another. If determining what our real defense needs are is too difficult and technical a problem for Congress to cope with, how can we expect that the average citizen will be better equipped? If asking taxpayers how much they want to spend on future wars is an example of the statesmanship we can expect from our legislators who want to reduce military spending, we are in for a very bad time. Building a ground swell of emotional antipathy to military defense by calculated gimmickry is not a way to exercise the responsibility of elective office and merely reinforces the prejudices of those who believe that defense is too serious a business to be left to politicians.

It is ironic that service rivalry, which in the forties and fifties was looked upon as the curse of our military organization, leading to all manner of waste and inefficiency, is now regarded by many members of Congress as an ideal to which

* *Ibid.*, p. 105.

we should return. The most able Secretary of Defense of the postwar period (Mr. McNamara) is cast as villain because he made the operations of the Defense Department so much more efficient that Congress finds it more difficult to challenge. In the sixties budgetary priorities were thrashed out within the Defense Department, and the Joint Chiefs of Staff and the civilian Secretaries then presented a united front to Congress. Previously, when the service chiefs appeared before Congress, each was still fighting for a larger slice of the budgetary pie and Congress felt a greater sense of power and participation in determining the final outcome.

It is, of course, the function of the executive branch to prepare the budget and to determine how much should be spent for defense. But Congress, which must appropriate the money, cannot place all responsibility for increases in defense spending at the door of the White House, especially when it has so often appropriated more funds than the President asked for. As long as the Vietnam War continues, there is not much that Congress can do to effect major economies, but thereafter it might indicate to the executive branch what level of defense spending it considered appropriate and resolve to return the budget if it exceeded that amount—unless the President could make an overwhelmingly compelling case for it. This would transfer some of the burden of reducing spending back on the executive branch; but first, of course, Congress must marshal a majority that is seriously dedicated to this purpose.

Given the limitations of Congress—its present committee system, its lack of expertise, the pressures and distractions its members are subject to—there is probably no alternative to assigning a fixed percentage of the total budget to defense and allowing the Defense Department to determine how it will be spent. Congress would not surrender its power of review, but would then become a referee instead of a rather incompetent and ineffectual judge. It could still challenge the desirability of particular priorities or weapons systems, especially—as in the case of ABM and MIRV—where important political issues were involved. In effect, this was the method used in the Eisenhower Administration. President Eisenhower, the retired general, set the defense budget in accordance with what his advisers believed the economy could bear and then ordered the Pentagon to meet it. President Kennedy, who is more kindly remembered by today's critics of our military posture, directed the military establishment to tell him what was needed and he would then decide whether the nation could afford it. As one would expect under this system, defense budgets rose markedly.

Emphasis has been placed here on the responsibility of Congress for controlling the military-industrial complex, on the grounds (a) that Congress has the ultimate power of the purse, and (b) over the past two decades (Vietnam aside) it has actually proven more vulnerable to upward pressures on the defense budget than has the executive branch. There is no reason to believe that substantially lower expenditures for defense would require impossible adjustments for the nation as a whole, but for particular states the impact could be severe, some would say disastrous. Thus there is a core of Senators and Congressmen who are under enormous pressure to maintain defense production. Presumably one reason the Senate has seized on the issue of reducing force levels in Europe is that it is popular though not necessarily sound, while curtailment of new weapons systems may be sound but not popular.

Parenthetically, it is perfectly true that we cannot and should not be expected to keep 300,000 troops in Europe forever. *The Economist* has pointed out that between 1950 and 1968 the combined GNP of our ten largest and most industrially advanced allies rose from less than half to nearly three-quarters that of the United States. Over the same period their combined spending on defense rose from 34 percent of the American figure to 39 percent in 1965, and then fell back to 29 percent, partly as a result of our increased spending in Vietnam.*

* *The Economist* (London), Feb. 21, 1970.

It would be convenient to surmise that this merely reflects the good sense of our allies, but the fact is that many of them would be terrified if we now withdrew substantial forces from Europe, though probably none (with the possible exception of Germany) would increase its forces in compensation. The reason is simply that each individual nation sees its contribution as relatively inconsequential and all believe their ultimate security rests with the United States. This in turn requires more than a token presence of American troops in Europe. Until we can persuade our allies to do more or induce the Russians to negotiate a mutual reduction of forces, the psychological consequences of a substantial American withdrawal would be very serious indeed.

Keeping the upper hand on the military-industrial complex, then, does not consist in ill-considered reduction of forces which constitute an important factor of deterrence. It does consist in questioning assumptions, in reducing inefficiency and profiteering in weapons development and procurement, and in having the political courage to make unpopular decisions. Whenever the Defense Department announces the elimination of unneeded bases in the United States, the cry goes up from Congress to cut the budget someplace else. The military-industrial complex is indeed a danger, not because it is a malevolent monster, but because it has a kind of inertial-guidance system built into it, and its aim is upward. We all share responsibility for seeing to it that the executive and Congress bend every effort to change its course.

THE CENTRAL INTELLIGENCE AGENCY

Understandably no aspect or agency of government has drawn so much fire as the CIA. A secret governmental organization is anathema to an open society and would be attacked by many regardless of performance. We cannot even begin to assess the performance of the CIA, because so little is known and what has become public generally pertains to its failures rather than its successes. Since the CIA does not and cannot reply to charges against it, all are free to see its dirty hand in whatever happens abroad that might appear to favor American interests. Many such events have occurred in which the United States played no part whatever. In other cases, where there was an exposure embarrassing to the CIA, some other agency of the government was often responsible. For example, the *Pueblo,* the eavesdropping ship captured by the North Koreans, was the responsibility of the National Security Agency, which is in charge of this kind of operation. The CIA is only one part of the American intelligence community.

In discussing the CIA it is important to distinguish between its two principal functions. The first and by far the greater part is the collection and analysis of intelligence, most of it gathered in entirely open ways. Obviously, to act responsibly our government must be informed. The State Department, the Defense Department and the three armed services each has an intelligence service, and one of the functions of the CIA is to coordinate the masses of information collected. After analyzing it (i.e., what do the facts mean? how reliable is a particular piece of information?), it must put it in a concise and usable form for those who will base decisions upon it. Such intelligence is not confined to matters which other countries may want to keep secret, but includes, say, estimates of India's forthcoming wheat crop or Europe's consumption of oil.

The necessity of this aspect of the CIA's work can hardly be questioned. Without it the conduct of foreign policy would be impossible. To be sure, it includes cloak-and-dagger work in that we do seek information which others do not want to give —such as the installation of Soviet missiles in Cuba. It includes the use of photographic satellites, without which arms control would be virtually impossible, since the Soviets remain unlikely to permit ground inspection; it includes monitoring open and coded radio transmissions; and it includes the use of agents, though these have been playing a declining role as other means of gathering intelligence have improved.

The other and more limited aspect of the CIA's work is more controversial: those covert operations designed to affect events in other countries. Many believe that this cannot be condoned under any circumstances whatever; others believe that we cannot deny ourselves the means employed by our antagonists. Either way, it is an unpleasant business and many would agree that on too many occasions it has been done badly or that it might better not have been done at all.

Nevertheless, there are some misunderstandings about the CIA which have made it seem more suspect than necessary. First, it is not an autonomous body without supervision, undertaking devilish tricks on its own authority. Where it has played an activist role, it has been authorized to do so by the President after consultation with the National Security Council. Furthermore, these operations have been kept under review by an independent body of senior officials responsible directly to the President. Whether they have been able to give as much time and study as are required, whether they, as well as officials of the CIA itself, have been as skeptical of long-continued operations as they ought to be, are valid questions. A project unduly prolonged will sooner or later be exposed—its "cover blown," as they say in the trade—thus defeating the aim of the project, in part if not entirely.

Secondly, in an open society such as ours, operations of any size or complexity can be kept secret only with the cooperation of the press and others. During the fifties and early sixties, the press withheld information which it had obtained from confidential sources or which, in the individual judgment of editors, would endanger national security. It is far less inclined to do so now with the changed climate of opinion since Vietnam. Thus the CIA is a good deal more limited in what it can accomplish secretly than it was, say, ten years ago. The arming and training of Meo tribesmen to fight the Pathet Lao and North Vietnamese in Laos probably would have remained a secret a decade ago. In the late sixties it was reported without compunction. The mood of the country and the attitude toward clandestine operations generally are so changed that perforce the CIA must be more discriminating in what it undertakes, knowing that its secret will not be long kept. Conversely, when the press reports that the CIA had no responsibility for the overthrow of Prince Sihanouk in Cambodia, it probably can be believed.

For many people, one of the surprises in the revelation of the CIA's clandestine support of student and other legitimate organizations was how many liberal and left-wing causes it had aided. It had been widely assumed that the CIA, as a major instrument of "the war against Communism," was also reactionary. Nor could some believe that the CIA would not have sought to influence organizations it was supporting, though no one has produced evidence that it did. One of course wishes that the legitimate and even essential purposes for which the money was given could have been handled in some other way. But it is sadly true that if the President, in the late forties or early fifties, had asked Congress for a fund to permit those organizations subsequently assisted by the CIA to be represented at international conferences and for other such purposes, he would have been laughed off the Hill. Even after the exposure of the CIA, no substitute was found. The sensible proposal that a public corporation comparable to the National Science Foundation be set up for this purpose has received no support. To be sure, from a national point of view the need is less acute today, but for the organizations affected by the exposure the mishandling of a valuable undertaking has meant not only anguish but often collapse.

The CIA can be faulted for instances of bad judgment or poor execution. But it cannot be criticized for doing what it was created by Congress to do and ordered by the Chief Executive to do. Though it has influence, the CIA is not an independent center of power, and since its inception, for all the secrecy surrounding it, it has been more in the public eye than any comparable organization in the world. Nowhere else, for example, is the head of a nation's clandestine service publicly and officially known. The CIA is a convenient whipping boy for the discontented both at home and abroad, but it is almost certainly a less dangerous and pernicious organization than it has been painted.

The institutions which have, or are imagined to have, power are numerous, and only a few can be examined here. Two others that deserve more objective study than they have received are business and the press. In recent years particularly, the press (including all news media) has demonstrated a frightening capacity to endow with power men and movements which would have had no significant following but for its arbitrary decision as to what constitutes front-page news. So it was that Senator Joseph McCarthy attained his undeserved prominence, and so it is today that those who preach hate and violence receive disproportionate attention. Publicity which could not be purchased at any price is free to those without a significant following or a program, providing they are sufficiently outrageous. Thus are "leaders" created, latent discontents inflamed and hatreds aroused. Here is a power which is unique, without check or balance. It is the power to endow with power those who might otherwise be ignored.

In an earlier chapter, we examined the power of American business operating abroad to disregard the interests of the United States and to involve it against its will. A more difficult question to assess is how much power business exerts in the formulation of American foreign policies generally. Many of the revisionist critics believe that commercial interests are the exclusive arbiter of our policies, that our political and even our military leaders are merely willing tools of the corporate structure. This seems an improbable hypothesis. Except in the field of trade, it is difficult to identify the impact of commercial interests, and even here there is of course no unanimity: some industries seek freer trade, while others demand protection. So in other areas, business rarely lines up on one side of an issue, and, partly in consequence, its impact on foreign policy is probably a great deal less than is supposed by the revisionists. For example, where we have intervened militarily in the postwar years, U. S. private investment was insignificant (with the exception of Cuba, where we intervened by proxy) and trade was unessential.

Unquestionably, American business has great influence, but its powers are heavily circumscribed by law, custom and the need for an acceptable public image. Reverting to the opening theme of this chapter, it is probably true to say that abroad American business has more power than influence, while at home, in the shaping of foreign policy, it has more influence than power.

The burden of this chapter is that power is not always what and where it seems, that the difference between power and influence is important and that both are much more broadly held in this country than is generally recognized.

XI

Toward a Balanced Appraisal

To KNOW where you want to go, it helps to know where you have been. For the young people of today whose political awareness does not go back beyond the beginning of our massive involvement in Vietnam, that war *is* American foreign policy. Little else exists save what reinforces that image of apparent uselessness and barbarity. For the rest, they are inclined to accept the judgment of older critics that our postwar foreign policy has been a failure. Our goals have eluded us, it is said, and security has not been achieved. The implication of this criticism is that the world's problems have final solutions or that failure to reach objectives means that they are ill-chosen. The first proposition is patently false and the second is not self-evident. That there is no security short of the grave is a truism of more than usual validity today, and it is going to remain so further into the future than anyone can see. No sooner do we begin fully to comprehend the nuclear problem than overpopulation and pollution emerge on our consciousness as mortal threats to security. Problems arise faster than they can be dealt with, much less solved, in the domestic no less than the foreign field.

Romain Gary has shrewdly observed that "of all people, the Americans are the least gifted for nonsolving problems. That is not a compliment—they are unable to exist with a thorn in their side. . . . Americans are in bad shape today because there are too many problems at once."*

If one finds our own mistakes and failures of foreign policy depressing, it is constructive to view those of the Soviet Union or China as they might be seen from Moscow or Peking. Let us imagine that we are Russians and Chinese candidly assessing our positions in the world.

The view from Moscow:

The unity of the Communist world which we were about to achieve slipped through our fingers, and the most populous nation on earth is now our mortal enemy. We are again surrounded by enemies. None of the countries of Western Europe has embraced Communism. Lenin insisted this was essential if the world movement were to succeed, and it seemed so imminent after World War II. If Stalin had appeared less aggressive, the United States might have returned to isolation and we would have become the dominant influence throughout Europe and quite possibly Asia. Barring that, we at least should have taken advantage of the Marshall Plan; to have accepted the offer would have embarrassed the United States and speeded our recovery. No country of consequence anywhere has adopted Communism, with the one exception of China, and we would be better off if it were still under Chiang. The irrationality of Mao's China and its emergence as a nuclear power are terrifying. Of almost all our undertakings in the postwar period it can be said that if we had been willing to settle for half a loaf we might have got it; by going after everything all at once, we excited so many fears that nearly the whole world has been arrayed against us. Our allies constantly threaten to abandon us for the temptations of the West, and we continue to be embarrassed by the need to deal with them by force. In Berlin we had to build a wall to stop the outward flow of skilled people and the inward flow of unpalatable ideas; yet

* Interview with John L. Hess in *The New York Times*, April 27, 1970.

Berlin remains the aggravation it has always been. We have failed to overtake the United States economically, as Khrushchev promised we would, and the cost of trying to equal or surpass it in weaponry is an ever-increasing burden. After a spectacular start in space, we fell behind and had to pretend we were no longer competing.

Despite our economic failures, we are looked upon by the Third World as fat cats, and no longer are we regarded as a revolutionary model with universal application. We must compete abroad not only with Western ideas of liberal democracy but with Maoism, Castroism, Trotskyism and several other bastard brands of Marxism-Leninism. We sank a billion dollars in Indonesia for absolutely no return, our generous aid to North Vietnam has bought us little influence, and Castro is no longer worth his cost to us. Indeed, having to pull our missiles out of Cuba was a humiliation which offset everything we had gained there. The Africans are impossible to organize or discipline, and after repeated failures we have had to liquidate most of our efforts there. We armed the Arabs at enormous cost and they blew the whole thing in six days. Now we have armed them again, only to lose—with the death of Nasser—the only Arab leader strong enough to be an effective instrument of our policies. Less than ever do we have adequate control of the situation to protect our interests and to avoid a war we do not want.

The view from Peking:

We have forever allowed domestic political considerations to get in the way of foreign policy, with the result that today we have virtually no influence anywhere except in Albania, of all places, and among a few wild-eyed revolutionaries here and there who have no discipline and no conception of what revolution is all about. In the middle fifties we were making enormous strides both at home and abroad; by professing allegiance to the spirit of Bandung we were gaining friends and influence everywhere, and our prestige throughout Africa and Asia was enormous. Our performance at home, the impressive growth of our economy, was winning us the respect of the world. Then the old man insisted that we become arrogant and insulting, even to our friends, while the Great Leap Forward and the Cultural Revolution made us look ridiculous in the eyes of the world. The failure of the Communist revolt in Indonesia was an unmitigated disaster. It might all have been different, too, if the Russians hadn't unleashed their man Kim Il Sung to invade South Korea. That brought the Americans into Asia to stay and it frightened the Japanese, making them far less amenable than they otherwise would have been. We've made no progress toward obtaining the return of Taiwan. The fantastic economic growth of Japan has shown what an Asian country can do and, compared with our bumbling, it hasn't done the reputation of Communism any good in Asia. With Japan's economic power allied to American military power, we are really boxed in. As though that weren't bad enough, we had to pick a fight with the Soviet Union which meant an end to all economic and technical assistance and a buildup of Soviet forces on our frontier that could wipe us out before we become a real nuclear power. Our occupation of Tibet assures us of hostility there, and, just to make sure we were wholly surrounded by enemies, we attacked India. Even in Indochina, things are not as good as they appear. The more successful the North Vietnamese are, the more they are likely to assert their independence of us and to usurp our rightful position of influence in Indochina. Meanwhile, they are playing us off against the Russians in a most ungrateful way. Also the war in Indochina has served to increase Soviet influence and activity in East and Southeast Asia. Things are not going well, and much of it is due to our own ineptitude.

Such assessments will of course arouse argument. Some will rightly point out that this is not in fact the way Moscow and Peking view the world. Some will say these hypothetical assessments grossly neglect Communist gains; others will say, If they are even remotely accurate, what are we so worried about? Still others might point out that, if these assessments have a grain of truth, the United States must have played some positive role in bringing them about. Unfortunately the validity or falsity of this contention cannot be proven, though both sides in the argument might concede that most countries make their own mistakes; they are not thrust upon them.

As negative an assessment of the position of the United States as those given for the Soviet Union and China would be difficult to draft and harder to make credible—though many have tried. The Western world is not coming apart at the seams; in many respects it is being knit together ever more closely, not by American dominance, but by common interests —now more economic than strategic. We have settled for the enemies we had and avoided making new ones. We have not antagonized all our neighbors and have not felt obliged to use force against our principal allies to keep them in line. If our authority is being more widely challenged, so much the better; the notion that we aspired to hegemony in Europe or anywhere else is without foundation. Despite the lessened predominance of the U. S. economy, the dollar is more important than ever in the international monetary system. The OECD countries (which means the industrialized nations of the West plus Japan) collectively exceeded their goal of 50 percent growth in GNP over the past decade. Our reputation abroad has been injured by the war in Vietnam, but the damage is not irremediable, especially as Hanoi's image as a heroic David is becoming less and less convincing as it plays the role of Goliath in Laos and Cambodia and as it rejects out of hand ever more reasonable terms for ending the war.

One of the constant refrains of alienated young people and intellectuals is that the government won't listen to them. What they mean, of course, is that the government won't comply with their wishes. Since they often represent a minority, this is not surprising. Democracy, Churchill once observed, involves "the occasional necessity of deferring to the opinions of others." What is surprising is that critics take so little account of what they have accomplished. It is not every day that a minority persuades a President of the United States in effect to resign. The course and direction of the war was altered, even if not sharply enough to satisfy the ever-growing minority. A little more historical perspective would have helped the protesters to understand that there was no precedent for their demands—for the United States to back out of a war without even a negotiated settlement. Seen in this light, their accomplishments seem more substantial than they realize, especially as the President was always able to hold a majority of opinion with him. It is significant, too, that when the protesters began to demonstrate less and reason more, politicians and officials listened more attentively.

Every age has had its dissenters; indeed, it used to be a lonely business. Rarely did they receive in a lifetime as much attention as a seventeen-year-old now can obtain in a week. Publishers compete for their work; television provides them with the opportunity to address the nation; the press covers their protests and virtually creates national figures by giving page-one attention to dissenters who in another time would have remained in obscurity. And no one is listening? Never did any society in history ever listen to its young so attentively. Traditional societies, where wisdom is a concomitant of age, find the seriousness with which we take our young utterly incomprehensible.

Those who have felt outraged by the unresponsiveness of government should remember, too, that high sensitivity to public opinion is not an unqualified virtue in government. A little less sensitivity to McCarthyism or the China Lobby—to take just two recent examples—would have been a good thing. In the context of Vietnam it may seem an affront to point out that many of the greatest acts of statesmanship have occurred when leaders had the courage to defy public opinion. But it is precisely at such traumatic times as these that we need to remind ourselves that the United States is a republic, not a pure democracy. Our elected officials are accountable to the public for their performance, but a foreign policy that was responsive to every domestic pressure would be no policy at all. This is not to defend Vietnam policy of any period, but merely to point out that responsiveness should not become an end in itself. It is a coin with two sides.

For as long as we have had representative government, it has been the despair of some that the principle of one man, one vote did not adequately take into account the intensity with which a point of view may be held. In the polling place, the voter who is disposed to give his confidence to the government because he sees no alternative counts as heavily as the voter who is passionately opposed to the government and is positive he knows a better policy.

Young people are right, of course, in feeling that politicians would be more inclined to heed their protests if the voting age were eighteen, as it should be. But this would not necessarily have been sufficient to alter policy more quickly or radically. For one thing, the impression that young people have been overwhelmingly against official policy in Vietnam has not been borne out by the opinion polls.* For another, in setting Vietnam policy American leadership consistently considered other factors more important than public opinion. What these other factors have been is a matter of speculation and dispute, but they are almost certainly more complicated than most dissenters suppose. For example, the decision to go into Cambodia surely cannot be explained simply as "a surrender to the generals" or as "proof that the President does not want peace."

In fact we do not know the real reasons for the Cambodian invasion and, though each of us is very sure whether it was right or wrong, only history will tell whether the decision was justified. And concern with their reputations in history is precisely what has motivated most Presidents when the going was rough. From this flows advantages and disadvantages. On the one hand, where vital issues are at stake Presidents are less

---

* A Gallup poll released March 14, 1970, indicated that only 18 percent of college students favored immediate withdrawal of all troops, compared to 21 percent for all adults.

likely to act out of political expediency. No matter how opportunistic they may have appeared as Presidential candidates, no matter how they may play politics in a variety of ways after gaining office, when it comes down to issues involving national security or basic national interests they generally follow their consciences in what they genuinely believe to be the best interests of the country. This may sound pious today, but historical observation bears it out. And it carries dangers as well as merits. The disadvantage of Presidents' concern with the esteem of future generations rather than with popularity in the present is that vanity may interfere with reason. Almost every President of the United States—at least those of any stature or who served in times of particular difficulty—has demonstrated both aspects of this concern with history: acts of political courage in making unpopular decisions and identification of the good of the nation with his own good repute in the perspective of time. Often the two occur together.

If this is true, then it affects the manner in which a President's mind can be changed. The more central the issue, the more resistant to pressure Presidents become. Threats of political retaliation cease to work. Demonstrations become counterproductive. This is not to say that these methods have no place or that they do not affect the environment in which decisions are made. But the only means of persuading a President to change his mind or his course of action on a vital issue is either to marshal a substantial majority of the people against him or to convince him to alter his assessment of the long-run national interest. This means persuading him to alter the values he has assigned to those myriad conflicting interests which can never be wholly reconciled and some of which cancel out others, but which must ultimately be toted up to reach a decision. It does no good to question his integrity or his intelligence, except as a means of gathering forces to defeat him, and this too may backfire. He, of course, has unrivaled means for keeping a majority of the people with him. So while a frontal assault on, say, a political appointment may be successful, it is unlikely to carry the day on a vital international issue where the President is dug in. And the more his opponents paint the issues in blacks and whites, the more resistant to argument he will become, for if there is one thing of which he is sure, it is that he actually faces nothing but grays.

In a broader context than that of Southeast Asia or the Presidency, Charles Frankel has articulated that difference in perspective which accounts for much of the tension between government official and outside critic. Of the latter he writes:

. . . There is a certain amplitude in his view of the world. He can think of it as pliable and amenable to the application of thought, and he can feel that with good will and intelligence all sorts of things can be arranged or rearranged. He lives at the opposite pole psychologically from the man for whom it is enough just to get through the working day in one piece.

But that is the life, in large part, of the State Department official. From where he sits—from where he runs—the world is less tractable, insanity and cruelty are at its very heart, and a day is a series of crises. And the immediate imperative, the game that he plays every day, is to get through each crisis in good enough condition to be able to face the next.

. . . Timing, the measurement of how much you can get away with at any particular moment, is an unavoidable imperative of official life. This is why an official may seem deaf when, in fact, he isn't. The man on the outside who has an idea or complaint usually has only that one idea or complaint on his mind at the time. But the official has a number of balls in the air. He is engaged in a juggling act. For him, the problem is not the simple one of deciding between doing the right thing and doing the wrong thing. The problem is to decide which of the beautiful balls in the air he will try to catch and which he will allow to fall to the ground.*

Understanding, even some compassion for those who bear the burdens of making decisions, is not inconsistent with

* Frankel, *High on Foggy Bottom* (New York: Harper & Row, 1969), pp. 137-40.

pointed criticism and a skeptical approach to government. It is unlikely that government will be affected or improved by those who embrace those very characteristics which they find so prevalent in American society: arrogance, self-righteousness, irrationality, deceit, lust for power, an unwillingness to listen, a lack of regard for the rights of others and a disposition to violence. Yet, with exceptions, these are the hallmarks of our extreme critics.

It is one of the truisms of our faith—or lack of faith—that people get the government they deserve. And this ancient saw may have a particular relevance to contemporary American politics. Although men have always believed that politicians were crooks and rascals, in our own country it has more often than not been expressed with a measure of humor in the tradition of the music-hall joke which allowed of exceptions. Moreover, to some degree it was the credo of the mass public far from the seats of power and predisposed to believe that those who represented them in Washington were robbing them blind. What distinguishes the cynicism of the present is that it extends to those who by education and position might be expected to be more discriminating in their judgment, and that it is applied to what collectively is probably the most able and most dedicated group of public servants this country has ever had. Those who have served in Washington in the past quarter century have been predominantly those who achieved some considerable degree of responsibility in World War II, at a time when public service was the ultimate good. Despite the McCarthy era, that tradition of public service is deeply embedded in the generation that is now past its middle forties. But what of the oncoming generation? How shall we staff our executive branch with a generation so many of whom believe —and have been taught to believe—that those in the most responsible positions of government are contemptible and motivated only by the quest for power, or that the system ultimately corrupts even the virtuous? Shall we then have a bureaucracy made up of those for whom personal ambition truly *is* the guiding motivation, without a sense of commitment or service? Those who teach the doctrine of inevitable corruption of government are placing a heavy mortgage on our future. For the power of government, which Americans have feared since colonial times, will not go away. It increases year by year as more demands are placed upon it, and it will be managed and controlled only with the active participation of our most concerned and selfless citizens.

The "cheap optimism" of an earlier age, Daniel Moynihan has written,

> has been replaced by a not less commonplace despair. Established institutions insist upon it. Fashionable university presidents, forward-looking churchmen, prestigious columnists revel in it. It has become the mark of the middling mind. . . . [The danger is that] relentless emphasis on what is wrong, what is worsening, what is threatening can lead a people to underestimate its capacity to control events. Politics comes increasingly to resemble what Lenin called an "infantile disorder." Society regresses to a state of complaining helplessness and threatened hysterics.

Aristotle said that "justice exists only among men whose mutual relations are governed by law." From his time until the American Revolution, every society in fact placed order above justice, stability above freedom. What made our War for Independence revolutionary was precisely this break with the tradition of ages, this reversal of established values. Since then we have been struggling with uneven success to reconcile freedom with justice and stability. For it was soon apparent that freedom did not insure justice, especially as both concepts changed over time—and at an ever-increasing pace today. It is ironic that a decade in which the search for greater freedom and justice has markedly accelerated should have ended in despair and disorder; the more so because our principal foreign antagonists, so much admired by those who condemn American efforts, still value order above justice, stability above freedom.

What Reinhold Niebuhr wrote in the decade of "the silent generation" seems even more relevant today:

Modern optimistic interpretations of the historical and political problem easily obscured the possibility both of destructiveness and of creativity in the growth of freedom. The historical development of freedom was believed to be purely creative, partly because it was believed that increasing freedom meant increasing rationality; and increasing reason was tantamount to increasing disinterestedness which would overcome both injustice and parochialism in the community. This was the burden of the "idea of progress." Unfortunately, the growth of freedom had more ambiguous consequences than the optimists assumed. Reason, despite every refinement, could always become the servant of interest and passion, even if the general tendency of rational growth was increasing disinterestedness. Reason also could become the servant of the parochial rather than of the ideal universal community. Thus, historical development did not solve any of the problems of the community. Instead, it constantly enlarged them until our generation faces these problems in a global dimension.*

And as though anticipating a generation which expects to accomplish everything between the ages of seventeen and twenty-five, Niebuhr concludes: "It is man's ineluctable fate to work on tasks which he cannot complete in his brief span of years, to accept responsibilities the true ends of which he cannot fulfill, and to build communities which cannot realize the perfection of his vision."†

The very success we have enjoyed in this country has taught us to be optimists. The tragedy we experience in our personal lives is seen as something individual and exceptional. But gradually the American people are learning—perhaps too abruptly —that our rational idealist view of the world is mistaken. They are learning that in many instances all our choices may be bad,

* Niebuhr, *The Structure of Nations and Empires* (New York: Scribner's, 1959), p. 289.
† *Ibid.,* p. 298.

yet we may not be able to escape making them; that not all problems have solutions, though we must go on seeking them; that not all conflicts can be negotiated, though we must never cease to try.

Edward Shills may be close to the truth when he points out that, while we have long believed that some earlier age was better than our own, now for the first time since the Enlightenment we no longer believe that a later age will be better than our own. We have lost our confidence in a better future. May this not be the root cause of our present dissatisfactions? Belief in a life hereafter, belief in the essential goodness and perfectibility of man, and belief in the inevitability of history, each in turn held out a hope which is now felt to be destroyed. Not only here but abroad, man is more frightened and uncertain than at any time since hell lost its reality. We are not likely to find a new sense of purpose until we have regained our self-confidence and our compassion. Meanwhile, we can hope that John Dewey's words yet apply: "It still remains true that the troubles which men undergo are the forces that lead them to project pictures of a better state of things."

The United States emerged out of two world wars in this century projecting "pictures of a better state of things." The first time we did nothing about it, and world war recurred in a generation. The second time we tried to give those pictures some reality, moved by a complex sense of opportunity, obligation and fear. To say that we have failed is to look at the picture in only one dimension, through the smoke of Vietnam. In longer perspective, we need not feel shame. What the world has to fear is not American domination but that out of disgust or internal dissension we will indulge ourselves in our historical and instinctual preference for withdrawal into our own mink-lined shell. Technically it would be difficult to disengage, but psychologically it would be easy, even natural. We are most likely to do so if we deprive ourselves of self-respect, as we seem intent on doing, even more by our words than by our actions. In that event we will not only play no constructive role in the world, we might very well fulfill the worst fears of those who proclaim us a dangerous and unpredictable nation. Let us instead cease the self-abasement, the assignment of blame, the spinning of theories of our iniquity, and get about the tasks that need doing.

Index

About the Author

PHILIP W. QUIGG brings to his brilliant study of American foreign policy of the last quarter century an expertise that few professionals can match. For fifteen years he was managing editor of *Foreign Affairs,* the most respected journal of its kind in the United States. In that position he dealt with most of the key policy-making officials of government as well as knowledgeable scholars. Thus, although he has been close to government, he has never been of it, and he has no axes to grind. In the course of his career, Mr. Quigg has traveled in some fifty countries. He has written reviews for *Book Week* and *The New York Times Book Review* and articles for many magazines as well as *Foreign Affairs.* He is the editor of *Africa: A Foreign Affairs Reader,* published in 1964. Mr. Quigg is a graduate of Princeton University, where he won high honors in the Woodrow Wilson School of Public and International Affairs. He and his wife reside in New York City.